THE HIGH SCHOOL COUNSELOR TODAY

THE HIGH SCHOOL COUNSELOR TODAY

A series of papers meant to instruct the beginning and practicing counselor in his counseling function and related activities

EDITED BY

THOMAS C. HENNESSY, S.J.

ST. PAUL EDITIONS

Library of Congress Catalog Card Number: 65-28758

Copyright, 1966, by the DAUGHTERS OF ST. PAUL

Printed by the DAUGHTERS OF ST. PAUL
50 St. Paul's Ave., Jamaica Plain, Boston, Mass. 02130

CONTENTS

PART I: THEORETICAL

PART II: PRACTICAL

9

10   CONTENTS

INTRODUCTION

Most of the papers which are collected here were originally prepared for the seventh annual Fordham University Guidance Institute. The seventh Institute was devoted to a study of "Program Development and Management Responsibilities of the School Counselor." Perhaps the sub-title of the Institute is more meaningful to some readers. It is "Organization and Administration of Guidance Services."

Some of the routine and less glamorous activities of the counselor were not discussed in the papers but were examined in the workshops which followed the papers. However, the omission of certain topics and the pattern that evolved in the final content of the volume seem to call for the title which is now on this book.

When the papers were collected, it seemed that they fell into two different types. The decision was reached to call the first type Theoretical and the second type Practical. One could readily disagree with this dichotomy, since there is much of the practical in the first part of the volume and much of the theoretical in the second part. At least it is clear that the more theoretical papers are in the first part and the more practical ones in the second.

Of course, thanks are due to many who shared in the work of producing this book, especially to each of the speakers who also edited their talks for publication, to the members of the panel discussion, and in a very particular way to Dr. Genevieve Hunter Loughran who planned and conducted the Institute in an extremely capable way and who provided the manuscripts of some papers delivered in earlier Institutes.

11

Special gratitude is due to the following: colleagues in the School of Education, particularly Rev. Philip H. O'Neill, S.J., Dr. Regis Leonard, Dr. Francis J. Crowley, Dr. Barbara W. Lake, Dr. Valda Robinson, and Dr. John M. Skalski as well as Rev. John W. Donohue, S.J., Dean of the Thomas More College for suggestions regarding the Counselor's Library; Anne M. Murphy, Associate Librarian of the Fordham University library and her staff—for research regarding the Counselor's Library; Sister Francis Lillian, Howard A. Kelly, Henry A. Mallon, and Florence V. Winter—for providing the original drawings of the counseling suites; Rev. Philip E. Dobson, S.J., and his friends in Perkins & Will, Robert H. Levine and Michel Senet—for the uniform professional drawings of Ruth Buescher and Carrie Gimpleson—for proof reading the galley sheets; the counseling suites; Peter J. Gallagher—for the attractive jacket design of the book; and finally—Mother Paula, D.S.P. and Sister Concetta, D.S.P. and their co-workers among the Daughters of St. Paul, for their indefatigable labor and vast patience with the many changes that preceded the printing of this book.

THOMAS C. HENNESSY, S.J.

March 17, 1966.

ABOUT THE CONTRIBUTORS

BROWN, NATHAN: Assistant Superintendent of Schools, Pupil Personnel Services, Division of Child Welfare, New York City. He received his doctorate at New York University. He is a former teacher, chairman of department, and principal in the New York City public high schools. He has also written a number of articles on guidance for the atypical child.

CARRON, REV. LIONEL V., S.J.: Psychological counselor, at the Psychological Services Center, University of Detroit. For many years he has been director of this center. He received his Master's degree at St. Louis University. His educational experiences include being principal of a high school, professor and administrator at the college level.

COHEN, ELI: Executive Secretary of the National Committee on Employment of Youth. He is an alumnus of the University of Illinois. He has concerned himself with the vocational problems of young people for over a quarter of a century as counselor, educator and executive in Chicago, Philadelphia and New York. He has been a consultant on youth employment to the U.S. Department of Labor and served as forum speaker and technical consultant at the 1960 White House Conference on Children and Youth.

COTTLE, WILLIAM C.: Professor of Education and Director of the Counselor Education and Counseling Psychology Program, Boston College. He received his doctorate at Syracuse University. Formerly he was a teacher, counselor and principal in New York State public schools, Professor of Education, University of Kansas, and president of the American Catholic Psychological Association and the National Vocational Guidance Association. His publications include: *The MMPI, a Review* (1953), *Procedures and Preparation for Counseling* (co-author) (1960).

DiMICHAEL, SALVATORE G.: Regional Representative of the Vocational Rehabilitation Administration. He received his doctorate at Fordham University. He has been Consultant in Psychological Services in the U.S. Office of Vocational Rehabilitation and was the first Executive Director of the National Association for Retarded Children. He has taught at the Catholic University of America and St. Louis University. He has been president of the American Rehabilitation Counseling Association, the Division on Psychological Aspects of Disability of the American Psychological Association, and the American Catholic Psychological Association. He was a member of the Editorial Board of the *Personnel and Guidance Journal*, edited *Vocational Rehabilitation of the Mentally Retarded*, and has published *Improving Personality and Study Skills in College* (1951), and over sixty articles and bulletins.

EWELL, ELIZABETH: Associate Supervisor, Bureau of Guidance, New York State Education Department. She did graduate work at New York State University at Buffalo and received her M.A. at Columbia University. Formerly she was teacher, dean of girls and director of guidance in New York State schools.

HENNESSY, REV. THOMAS, C.S.J.: Assistant Professor, School of Education, Fordham University. His area of instruction is guidance and counseling. He received his doctorate at Fordham University. Formerly he was a high school teacher and guidance counselor. He has edited *The Inner Crusade* (Loyola University Press, 1965).

KLOPF, GORDON: Associate Chairman, Guidance Programs Bank Street College of Education. He received his doctorate at the University of Wisconsin. Formerly he was a high school teacher and a university dean of students. His publications include: *College Student Government* (1960), *Interns in Guidance* (co-author) (1963), *Integration in the Urban School* (1964).

LOUGHRAN, GENEVIEVE HUNTER: Associate Professor, Hunter College. She received her doctorate at St. John's University. Formerly she was the Director of the New York Archdiocesan Vocational Service, president of the New York City Personnel and Guidance Association, and Associate Professor, School of Education Fordham University.

RICCIO, ANTHONY C.: Associate Professor of Education, Ohio State University. He received his doctorate at Ohio State University. Formerly he was an Assistant Professor, Notre Dame University. His publications include: *Organization and Administration of Guidance Services* (co-author) (1962), *Teaching in America* (ed.) (1962), *Guidance in the Elementary School—A Book of Readings* (co-author) (1963)., *Teaching in the American Secondary School* (co-author) (1964)

SHEAR, BRUCE E. Director, Division of Pupil Personnel Services, New York State Education Department. He received his M.S. at Syracuse University and has had additional graduate education at Teachers College Columbia University. He has been a public school teacher, vice-principal, counselor, guidance director, director of pupil personnel services and college teacher. He has been a consultant to the U.S. Office of Education Department and the Chicago School Survey. He has held the office of president in the Association for Counselor Education and Supervision and in the New York State Association of Pupil Personnel Administrators. He has been a member of the APGA Executive Council and of the editorial board of *Counselor Education and Supervision.*

THOMAS, SISTER MARY, O.P.: Coordinator of Guidance, Diocesan High Schools, Diocese of Brooklyn, and adjunct Assistant Professor, Fordham University. She received her doctorate at Fordham University. Formerly she was a teacher and director of guidance in high school.

WILLIAMSON, EDMUND G.: Dean of Students, and Professor of Psychology, University of Minnesota. He received his doctorate at the University of Minnesota. He is a regular contributor to the major guidance periodicals. His books include: *How to Counsel Students* (1939), *Trends in Student Personnel Work* (1949), *Counseling and Discipline* (co-author) (1949), *Student Personnel Services in Colleges and Universities* (1961), *Vocational Counseling* (1965).

YANITELLI, REV. VICTOR, S.J.: President, St. Peter's College, Jersey City, New Jersey. He received his doctorate at Fordham University. Formerly he was a high school and college teacher and Vice President for Student Personnel, Fordham University, and Director of Student Personnel, St. Peter's College. Recently he has been the president of the National Association of Student Personnel Administrators.

Part I:
THEORETICAL

PUPIL PERSONNEL SERVICES AND GUIDANCE

BRUCE E. SHEAR

Director, Pupil Personnel Services
New York State Education Department

As a means of establishing a sound foundation for the current activities of guidance, Mr. Shear examines a number of issues which are fundamental to the guidance movement. Among these are aspects of the philosophy underlying guidance and the relationship of guidance to other pupil personnel services. In his discussion of pupil personnel services he offers an excellent summary of the philosophy and present division of work in this field. Furthermore he provides the most recent data concerning the staffing of pupil personnel services in the New York State public schools.

There has been much talking and writing lately about the need to give more attention to the "why" in guidance, particularly guidance in schools. In this paper I wish to develop briefly two themes with "why" implications.

PHILOSOPHY OF SCHOOL GUIDANCE

Recent Trends

At present there is a tendency in many quarters to search for a philosophy of guidance. There are some who strongly support the notion that guidance in the past has functioned and presently continues to function in schools without a philosophy. They say that it lacks a set of basic underlying enunciated principles.

At the recent APGA convention in Chicago, as part of the program of the Association for Counselor Education and Supervision, a major paper was presented on guidance philosophy and objectives. In the paper particular attention was given to the nature of values and the nature of man. [1] Careful consideration of these two areas is, of course, very important in searching for the "deeper why" behind education and guidance in education. However, this is a courageous but sometimes tenuous approach. The converse of the "deeper why" for some, so often appears to others to be the "deeper why." Or, to put it another way, some old and abiding "whys" have a deeper meaning for many than do "whys" advocated by some who see them as deeper merely because they are more recently expounded.

In responding at the convention to this position paper, I indicated that had I approached the task of preparing such a paper, my frame of reference would have been tied very closely to present concepts of the philosophy and objectives of elementary and secondary school education and the guidance roles within this context. In my opinion there is already a sound and dynamic philosophical basis for school guidance, that is, considerable "why" in support of both guidance policy and practice.

A Constant Thread

Looking back over about thirty years of personal experience related to school guidance, it seems to me that one trend has been that the developing policy has been constantly challenged and pulled off center in one direction or another. This is perhaps not unexpected or undesirable in a young and emerging field, but for those who do not see the continuing and quite constant threads of "why" running throughout this period, these deviations can be confusing and disconcerting. It leads them to wonder what the real "why" is and to discount the continuing presence of well developed and useful guiding principles.

More directly, what I am referring to here is the persistent emphasis which has characterized school guidance development over the years. To me this continuing and desirable core of direction has been and still should be the idea of assistance to all pupils in planning and progressing educationally in definite preparation for occupational competence and contribution.

Along the way this emphasis in school guidance has survived many movements, has borrowed from them, but has continued, with increasing breadth and depth, to provide the kind and extent of guidance service which is compatible and supportive of school functioning and very much in line with the expressed desires of both pupils and their parents.

Different Emphases

Now digressing, from the "why" to the "what" area, I am concerned with the fact that we can point to only limited and partial implementation in schools of many areas of well conceived and carefully considered guidance practice. During the years of guidance development there have been periods of heavy emphasis on one practice or another. We have had a cumulative record period, a group guidance period, a follow-up study period, and many others. In each case considerable attention has been given to the "why" underlying the need for and development of the particular practice, the "what." In each case, however, after minor and limited flurries of implementation at the program level, we have jumped into the next period with all too little solid accomplishment in the given area on which to build further improvement in program practices. In addition, persons entering the field after a given period of practice emphasis has waned, seem to have been given in training too little appreciation of the background and bases which prompted the emphasis and influenced the development of the practice. Again and again, as is probably characteristic of our immaturity, we turn our major attention to new areas of practice without consolidating or continuing the gains in an area of earlier development.

Common Basic Principles

As previously noted, very often those who write about guidance put forward the idea that there is little guidance philosophy on which to base practice. Somewhat in contrast, my inclination is to support the contention that the more mature guidance educators and practitioners have worked, with a considerable degree of assurance, within a framework of basic or underlying principles which has given their guidance teaching or practice a well deserved recognition and acceptance, both professional and public.

There is no question but that there must be continued search for meaning, ceaseless and careful testing of theory, demonstration and implementation of proven practice. All of this, accelerated to be sure, should have a sense of direction not restricted to, but nevertheless well grounded in, present and past concept and practice. The process of refinement, replication, extension, and examination, constantly repeated, is more appropriate to school guidance improvement than repeated repudiation and rebuilding on a new and untested foundation.

In presenting principles which underlie school guidance, I am not going to explore the distant past nor try to tie the principles to present systems of philosophy. Mathewson, [2] Miller [3] and Wrenn [4] have been particularly helpful in exploring such roots and relationships. They have been, and are being, expressed over and over by school guidance personnel, guidance educators and supervisors. They also find frequent expression in the more general writings on elementary and secondary education and in other materials devoted to promoting a fuller understanding and development of children and youth through education. White House Conferences, President's Commission on Higher Education, Wolfle, Ginzberg, Conant, Educational Policies Commissions are sources of information and inspiration related to guidance.

Terms: Guidance versus Counseling

Perhaps you have noted the fact that I have not yet used the terms counseling or counselor but have talked only of guidance. This is quite in contrast to the thinking of some who would drop the use of the term guidance altogether. On occasion I too have thought this might be easier than defining its meaning and use. Now, however, I hold to its use because I sense a greater confusion and danger in the substitution of the term, counseling, to designate the school oriented concept and program in question. This is particularly the case when the school guidance program, or what is termed the major phase of it is conceived by some to be "Counseling" with a capital C and psychology added, that is, Counseling Psychology. Implementation of this idea, or even this approach, has implications for counselor education and school counseling practice which are overdrawn and in some respects quite incompatible with the function and role of the school counselor, today or for many tomorrows.

It is time, then, to turn to the underlying principles, the often recurring basic ideas, more and more commonly understood, which contribute a philosophical framework for school guidance program development. In short, these are the things "I" believe as "I" approach and carry out "my" role as a counselor in a school guidance program. These are also important considerations in formulating the objectives and criteria for the educational programs to prepare personnel for the school guidance responsbilities of school counselor and guidance director or supervisor.

I Believe

First, the individual pupil has a need of continuing and cumulative assistance in understanding his own capabilities in relation to opportunities and requirements of present and possible future environments, in making wise choices and plans for self-realization combined with social contribution, and, in makng satisfactory progress toward realistic and challenging goals. The reasons for this need for assistance and the factors influencing provisions for it are many. They include the concepts of: the worth, dignity, and uniqueness of the individual; the recognition and understanding of cultural differences; the individual's innate desire for acceptance and accomplishment and his inherent freedom of choice. Also involved are such factors as: our complex technological society; the diversity of educational opportunities; the social need for full development of all human potentialities; and, our national need for an increasing supply of highly educated and skilled manpower.

Second, the guidance program is an integral part of the total school program. What we have called the guidance point-of-view is becoming more and more the point-of-view of education in our democracy. All school staff members should participate and contribute in the program and the use and proper manipulation of the school environment in relation to the pupil can be a productive guidance technique. Actually the guidance environment of the pupil should be the whole school, and out-of-school, not just the counselor's office.

The school, well oriented and well ordered in terms of guidance, is in a unique position, in relation to effective developmental guidance, of having long-range and many faceted contacts with the pupil. The longitudinal picture which can be developed of the pupil's growth through education should be far more meaningful than mere cross-sectional glimpses of his potentialities. In addition, the school's opportunity to have a continuing cooperative relationship with parents can add immeasurably to the effectiveness of the guidance progress.

As an integral part of the school program, guidance information and guidance insights should be available to and used by administrators and teachers in providing bases for school program planning too meet individual and group needs. Also, the effectiveness of the guidance program contribution to the better understanding of pupils, to assistance in pupil planning, and to pupil progress should be studied and evaluated constantly.

In summary of this theme, the basic principles for guidance development, guidance is a process in education of assisting all pupils to understand themselves better, to profit from the opportunities of their environments, to relate well to others and to prepare for social competence and contribution. In schools the guidance areas of primary concern are those of educational planning and progress. These in turn, support the areas of career planning, occupational orientation and adjustment. Guidance attention, within the range of the normal problems of children and youth, is given to personal and social adjustments relating to education and career development. These concepts, then, are my set of basic principles. They give me the "why" needed for the development, extension and improvement of school guidance programs. Far from being restrictive, they provide the basis for a program of definite and needed scope and of unique and great contribution.

PUPIL PERSONNEL SERVICES AND GUIDANCE

The second theme to be developed here concerns the location of guidance within the structure of a school system. Present trends in school organization place guidance as one of the component parts of the pupil personnel program. Other parts of this program usually include attendance, health service, school psychological and school social work services. In this program the functions and activities of each part must be well defined, generally understood and carried out in relation to those of the other services.

Common Characteristics

All of the pupil personnel services are professional, educational services, functioning as an integral part of the total school program. The common objective of each service and of the overall pupil personnel program is to facilitate the maximum development of individual potentialities through education. All of these services offer direct assistance to pupils; they all function to assist teachers and parents in their teaching and personnel responsibilities and roles; and, all of them make use of appropriate out-of-school resources. The pupil personnel program is supportive of, but in the main distinct from, the program of classroom instruction. With adequate provisions for coordination among these services, and between them and other parts of the school program, the pupil personnel program becomes one of three interrelated phases of the school operation, instruction, administration, and pupil personnel.

Common Concepts

Certain concepts are basic to the proper functioning of a program of pupil personnel services. The first applies as well to all other phases of school operation. All of them apply equally to each of the separate services.

1. The worth, dignity and uniqueness of each pupil must be recognized and understood. Although this concept has already been expressed in the paper, it bears repeating here.
2. Pupil personnel services in the school setting function with an educational orientation. They are not considered

as clinical services and the remedial aspects of their work
are in support of the educational purposes of the school.

3. In content and process the pupil personnel program serves
   all pupils.
   a. The content of pupil personnel is the information con-
      cerning the unique qualities of the pupil, as these relate
      to environmental demands and
   b. The process of pupil personnel is developmental, pupil
      growth in self-direction through understanding of self
      in relation to environment.

4. The pupil personnel program recognizes the central role
   of the teacher in the educational development of the pupil
   and the responsibilities of the administration for the total
   school program.

5. The pupil personnel program recognizes the responsibility of the parent for the development of his child and
   does not function to supplant this responsibility nor to
   duplicate community responsibilities for assistance to
   the family.

Common Functions

The need for clear definition of the functions of each of the
pupil personnel services has already been mentioned. However,
in any such process it will become quite apparent that there are
many elements common to the work of several or all of the separate services. These might be listed and described briefly as
follows:

1. Appraising pupils, including case study, case conferences,
   and other types of comprehensive evaluation.

2. Providing and interpreting information about pupils.
       To pupils for self-understanding
       To parents and teachers to help them in assisting
          teaching processes, and
       To appropriate others for their use in aiding pupil
          development.

3. Providing and interpreting information concerning the influences, opportunities and demands of the pupil's environment. This information is provided, when appropriate
   to the pupil, his parents, and to school staff members.

4. Counseling, that is, assisting the pupil in decision making, self-direction, and self-realization.

5. Making use of and facilitating the use of out-of-school resources.

6. Referring to other in-school resources; preparing pupils and parents for referral to out-of-school resources.

7. Providing information and insights useful in planning the total school program and in highlighting the need for community referral resources.

8. Interpreting pupil personnel concepts and functions, and the roles of school staff members and parents in the pupil personnel program.

9. Cooperating in a pupil personnel team approach to the study of and assistance to pupils, inservice education, and assistance in curriculum planning.

10. Reporting on and evaluating pupil personnel activities and program effectiveness.

The point of referring to these common elements is not to encourage or imply the desirability of working toward the "homogenization" of the entire professional preparation or all of the functions within the area of pupil personnel. In this state, school district pupil populations are becoming larger and more varied, and educational problems are becoming more complex. Then, too, administrative units are increasing in size and this, along with administrative arrangements for sharing specialized services, makes specialization desirable and possible.

Under these circumstances, the strength of a pupil personnel program is built in two ways. The first of these is the development of strong programs carried out by competent, highly trained specialists in each field: attendance, guidance, school health, school psychological, and school social work services. The second is the provision for competent administration and supervision of the total program. The first provides for varied approaches to both common and unique elements within the pupil personnel program. The latter allows for approaches of varying degree and kind to the common elements of functioning, encourages the unique contributions of each specialty and coordinates the program of all services in a pupil personnel team approach in assistance to pupils and school program planning.

Now, following this presentation of ideas about pupil personnel concepts and program, let me describe in capsule form the objectives of the various services and indicate the present status of pupil personnel program coordination in the public schools of New York State.

Members of the Pupil Personnel Team

Attendance services should be provided to assure the identification of all pupils, including the handicapped, who will be or should be in school, to promote good school attendance, to accurately account for pupil attendance, absence, exemption or employment certification, and to seek out and help remedy the causes of non-attendance.

Good guidance, and enough of it, means that the guidance efforts of teachers and parents should be assisted and supplemented by an adequate number of trained counselors in order to assure the early identification of pupils' abilities, aptitudes, interests and educational needs, to provide assistance to all pupils in understanding of self in relation to educational and career opportunities and requirements, and to make available the help pupils need in setting the progressing toward realistic goals.

School health services, with an aim of bringing each child into optimum condition to profit from the educational program, should provide for annual health examinations and adequate follow-up, day-to-day health service and counseling, resource assistance to teachers in health teaching, and the maintenance of pupil health records, and in all of this, definite provision should be made that these health service activities be learning experiences for pupils.

School psychological and school social work services are provided to identify pupil needs and problems, to furnish diagnostic and case-study information as an important basis for remedial programs, to assist pupils with problems of educational, personal and social adjustment and to help the school staff gain deeper insights into the psychological and social needs of pupils in relation to effective learning and optimum development.

Data on Pupil Personnel Services in New York State

Since 1962 the Guidance Program Card which was distributed to school districts included a section "for use by the Division of Pupil Personnel Services." Information was requested on the name and title of any "person assigned to be in charge of the district-wide program of pupil personnel services." Districts were also asked to check services included in such an assignment. Attendance, guidance, school health, school psychological and school social work services were the categories listed.

The information which follows, then, is derived from the 1962-66 returns from the school districts of the state. The figures do not include cases where the superintendent, district principal, or supervising principal was designated on the returned form as the coordinator of pupil personnel services.

TABLE 1

**New York State School Districts Reporting
Persons Assigned to Pupil Personnel Coordination**

Number of services included in coordination	Number of Districts	
	1962-63	1965-66
2	20	30
3	23	44
4	53	76
5	24	40
Total	120	189

In 1962-63, one hundred of the 120 persons assigned district-wide administrative responsibilities for pupil personnel services carried out this responsibility for three or more of the pupil personnel areas. In 1965-66, the statistics were increased to 159 of the 189 persons assigned to pupil personnel coordination. In 1962-63, fifty-three of the persons had district-wide responsibility for four pupil personnel areas, and 24 persons had such an assignment involving five of the areas. In 1965-66, the statistics increased to 76 persons with four areas and 40 persons with five areas of responsibility.

In about three-fourths of these districts, the person assigned the district-wide responsibility for administration of pupil personnel services has a "pupil personnel" title, such as coordinator, director, or assistant superintendent of pupil personnel services. Between one-fourth and one-third of these persons have the additional assignment of an administrative responsibility in the area of education of the handicapped. In districts too small to warrant a full time assignment of coordination of pupil personnel services, this latter combination seems to be the one most often in effect.

In summary, one hundred and twenty persons were reported to have district-wide responsibilities for pupil personnel administration in 1962-66. Of these, the greatest number (76) are responsible for four of the pupil personnel areas within the district. Guidance and school psychological services are almost always included in such an assignment, with attendance, and school health services so included in about three fourths of the districts. At the present time, then, a "typical" school district assignment for administration of pupil personnel services includes coordinative and supervisory responsibility for attendance, guidance, school health and school psychological services. School social work service, where it exists, is usually included in the coordinated pupil personnel program. An indication of the trend toward pupil personnel program coordination in the public schools of the state is the growth from 120 to 189 of such specific assignments during the last three years.

It seems appropriate to indicate the growth in the guidance personnel in the public schools of New York State. Incidentally, no information is currently available concerning guidance personnel in private schools. The table which follows shows the increase both in terms of absolute numbers and in the pupil-counselor ratio.

TABLE 2

Time	1942	1948	1958	1962	1965
Full-time	75	175	1075	1945	2455
Part-time	650	700	750	313	430
Full-time equivalent	250	450	1400	2170	2635
Pupil-Counselor Ratio	1900:1	700:1	450:1	360:1	338:1

Two statistics in Table 2 to merit special notice. The first is the great increase in the number of full-time counselors in the period from 1942 to 1965: an increase of 2380 counselors. The second is the improved pupil-counselor ratio: from 1900 pupils to 338 pupils to the one counselor.

Recommendations

These pupil personnel concepts and trends lend added emphasis to the necessity for a definite and delimited focus and a clear understanding of guidance, and of every other part of the total pupil personnel program. It is time that we stop referring to "guidance and pupil personnel" and especially stop saying, as some textbook authors are inclined to do, that the terms guidance and pupil personnel are being used interchangeably. The overall program is pupil personnel, and guidance is one of the parts. Also, within the guidance program, counseling is only one of the parts.

As yet there are all too few clear statements and comprehensive treatments of topics in the area of pupil personnel services. Textbooks have been written, some of which serve as much to confuse as to clarify. Two of the most recent publications which ought to be brought to your attention are *Responsibilities of State Departments of Education for Pupil Personnel Services.* [5] and *A Rationale and Models for Organizing and Administering Programs of Pupil Personnel Services.* [6] While both of these are brief and neither of them is intended to tell the complete and final story, they are useful documents in clarifying concepts and pointing direction. In addition, there is at present, an Interdisciplinary Commission on Pupil Personnel Services with funds to conduct research and demonstrations in pupil personnel organization and practices. The work of this group should be very helpful in plotting the direction of the future in this area.

I have tried to develop two themes, quite interrelated, which have strong implications for guidance policy and practice. The first of these is that guidance is a clearly identified and necessary process in education based on a set of principles which have had and will continue to have an orderly and thoughtful development. The second theme has to do with guidance as one unique part of the overall pupil personnel program.

The full and effective implementation of these ideas and trends will require highly competent and well prepared, specialized personnel in each of the pupil personnel areas. In addition, personnel must be prepared and employed for administrative leadership and professional supervision of the total pupil personnel program.

REFERENCES

1. *Counselor Education - A Progress· Report on Standards*, Washington, D.C.: American Personnel and Guidance Association, 1962.

2. Mathewson, R.H. *Guidance Policy and Practice* (3rd ed.). New York: Harper and Row, 1962.

3. Miller, C.H. *Foundations of Guidance.* New York: Harper and Row, 1961.

4. Wrenn, C.G. *The Counselor in a Changing World.* Washington, D.C.: American Personnel and Guidance Association, 1962.

5. *Responsibilities of State Departments of Education for Pupil Personnel Services.* Washington, D.C.: Council of Chief State School Officers, 1960.

6. Lowe, R.N. *A Rationale and Models for Organizing and Administering Programs of Pupil Personnel Services.* Eugene, Oregon: University of Oregon, 1962.

FOR FURTHER READING

Ferguson, D.G. *Pupil Personnel Services*. Washington, D.C.: The Center for Applied Research in Education, 1963.

Sites, W. and Farrar, Marcella S. *Toward Better Adjusted Children*. Cleveland: Welfare Federation, 1957.

The Team Approach in Pupil Personnel Services. Hartford, Conn.: Connecticut State Department of Education, 1955.

BUT THE COUNSELOR
DOES SIT IN JUDGMENT

E. G. WILLIAMSON

Dean of Students and Professor of Psychology
University of Minnesota

The statement that "The counselor should not sit in judgment" of his counselees has often been made. In challenging this idea, Dean Williamson raises related issues. In the counseling process does he teach? Does he seek to impart attitudes, ideals and values? Should he try to be neutral about attitudes, ideals and values, even though he knows that research shows that he cannot be successful in this neutrality? Among those who hold to the "non-directive" position, the necessity of the counselor's being "non-judgmental" and his offering "unconditional acceptance" to the counselee is often stressed. Dean Williamson asks if this acceptance is unlimited in scope. His carefully reasoned analysis merits several readings and should provoke considerable thought regarding its implications. His stress on the need for objective standards will be applauded by many.

In addressing a recent institute for school counselors, something I said triggered the rejoinder: "We have been told that the counselor should not sit in judgment of the student." This remark has stimulated me to examine its implications and the possible reasons behind it. While I have not yet learned the logic underlying this particular formulation, yet it resembles others of similar import. Perhaps such an *obiter dictum* arises out of the concept-assertion that the counselee should be accepted "unconditionally," as Rogers worded it. [1]

One is justified in querying: Are there no limits to the acceptance of individuality? [2] Are any and all forms of individual actualization equally "good"? Probably the answer is "no" be-

34

cause Rogers hypothesizes that, if accepted unconditionally, the individual will "want" (need?) to become his "full" potentiality of humanity (a "fully functioning" individual). That is, it seems to be assumed that the "best" of one's potentiality will result (be produced by) from unconditional acceptance.

Several implications readily come to mind for examination and, hopefully, for understanding:

1. To be sure, most counselors would, perhaps, conclude from their counseling experiences that *not* to give evidence of *some* kind of degree of acceptance of the client would produce withdrawal, resistance and would also make effective rapport impossible or at least difficult to attain. And thus little, if any "good" results will be obtained in the counseling relationship, if the counselee perceives that he is "rejected" or at least not accepted in some degree. In this sense all counselors daily practice acceptance as an operational hypothesis of the order "If this— then that."

But the "non-evaluative," "non-judgmental" component of "acceptance" poses still another problem. Argyris phrases this point in these words, which equate "acceptance" with "non-evaluation" of the client.

> One way to minimize the probability of creating defensiveness in self, or in others, is to give feedback that describes a relationship without placing a value judgment on it. We call this *descriptive non-evaluative* feedback because it attempts to describe and not evaluate. [3]

But non-evaluative acceptance is difficult to achieve, apparently Argyris, in part at least, negates his admonition concerning the non-evaluation component when he goes on to state:

> For example, there is a significant difference between saying, 'you shouldn't behave in X manner,' and 'I experience the following feelings when you behave in X manner.' [4]

Surely the latter technique or relationship is not free of evaluation but is rather a more subtle and indirect manner of expressing evaluation persuasively through the use of *apparently* descriptive terms, calculated to avoid resistance. In some respects, the difference in the two phrasings parallel the use of argumentation and exposition in debate in contrast with techniques of persuasion. That is, both techniques of relationship are ways of evaluating but they differ in their side effects, one sometimes triggering resistance and resentment, and the other often *inducing a desire* to change one's behavior. But surely both phrasings are designed to "control" (manipulate?) behavior.

The past two decades or more have centered attention upon the ethics of influence as though to be thus indirect would be an ethical influence, whereas direct or frankly (honestly) identified influence was unethical. But without employing the criterion of ethics, we can examine the results of both techniques: the one is less effective in influencing human development, producing resentment and resistance, whereas the other induces desired and desirable development of the student.

And, moreover, I confess I have difficulty conceiving of any human relationship which is completely non-influential (either negative or positive) and also, therefore, non-evaluative, non-judgmental.

2. Assuming that Rogers' "unconditional" acceptance is similar to Maslow's, then we may postulate the corollary that both therapists perceive themselves as instrumentalities to be used by the client to achieve whatever goals in his life style he aspires to achieve; but they also assume that thus "unconditionally" accepted, he will want to and will become his full potentiality. Rogers explicitly stated such an expectant hypothesis in these words:

> I dare to believe that when the human being is free to choose whatever he values, he tends to value those objects, experiences and goals which make for his own survival, growth, and development, and for the survival and development of others. I hypothesize that it is *chacteristic* of human organism to prefer such actualizing and socialized goals when he is exposed to a growth-promoting climate. [5]

Maslow characterizes

the group of thinkers who have been working with self-actualization, with self, with authentic humanness, etc., have pretty firmly established their case that man has a tendency to realize himself.... They have *implied* without making explicit that if you can behave authentically, you *will* behave well, that if you emit action from within, it will be good and right behavior. What is very clearly implied is that this inner core, this real self, is good, trustworthy, ethical. [6]

Maslow goes on to assert his belief that this inner "good" will prove to be true but that it is not yet proved.

I have elsewhere examined this prior assumption that students will thereby aspire to become the "best" of their human potentiality. [7] To repeat, I have not yet become convinced that the Roussean notion of the innate "goodness" of man is justified by the record in all cultures of some men's inhuman and bestial treatment of some men. Indeed I conclude (tentatively and, nevertheless, hopefully, to be sure) that for some of us a lifetime of learning to *become* humane would seem to be required before there is "goodness" to be appealed to or "released" by means of acceptance.

And I note that Maslow acknowledges that besides acceptance, "other prerequisite conditions must also be satisfied." [8] Such conditions need to be clearly delineated. But one prerequisite or necessary condition is clearly delineated by Maslow in sharp contrast with Rogers' universal generalization to *all*: "Only to the self-disciplined and responsible person can we say, "do as you will, and it probably will be all right." (*Op. cit.*, p. 133).

One American philosopher makes a supporting relevant point of reservation concerning some forms of self-actualization:

> Consider, for instance, the plausible statement that the good life consists in self-actualization, in realizing one's total potentialities. Yet this man may have the potentiality of becoming a thief and this other man is an expert forger. We must distinguish between good and bad potentialities. [9]

To be sure, as is no doubt the case of all deans of students who perforce must "counsel" both the deviates (however defined) and the "good" students (also variously defined), I, too, have delightfully observed those with "peak" humanness. I have elsewhere, nevertheless, summarized much, but not all of my own counseling experience by expressing doubt that the "best" (however defined by whomever) will *necesasrily,* in and of itself, be the result of unconditional acceptance. I have cited my counseling efforts over several decades with two groups of college students who "chose" ("needed," i.e. low-achievement-need) to become less than their full potential; the disciplinary cases and the high ability underachiever. I acknowledge, that it is, of course, a tenable alternative explanatory hypothesis that I have not fully attained "unconditional" acceptance in my efforts to counsel.

3. Argyris says in a footnote (p. 18) that "positive feedback may be used to control individuals." Presumably control in this context seems to imply forced conformity. And Rogers has stated his reservation, if not opposition, to the attempt of one individual to control another,[10] perhaps on the grounds of the perplexing but rational query—who knows what is "best" for other persons? As an aside, perhaps such a philosophical and ethical query (the nature of the "good life") is indeed the dynamic thrust of organized human existence itself, indeed of the quest for self-actualization.

I wish to examine two points:

(a) Is not acceptance itself one means of "control" (manipulation)?" And is it always, in all cases, an effective means at that, as Rogers and Maslow seem to postulate? (Who keeps and publishes his own "success-failure score," in the use of any technique of counseling, is a much neglected but relevant question concerning all generalizations about all counseling techniques.)

(b) Is it contended that control-influence, of one by another, is necessarily "bad" or undesirable or harmful?

The first question seems answerable only as "yes" as I argued under (1) above (p. 35). And the kind of acceptance indicated by the modifier, unconditional, needs delineation and delimitation. Maslow makes a similar point in these words: "What answer must be given to the rapist or sadist who asks, 'Why should I too not trust and express myself?' "[12] In searching for answers to these questions, which imply some kind of criteria or standards of human conduct, external to the Rousseau "natural" man, I am reminded of Conant's *obiter dictum* that we need not (should not?) equate cannibalism (a form of self-actualization that deprives others of their right to self-actualization) or cruelty with the "good life." [13]

As to my second question concerning the "good" or "bad" of control of other individuals, I raise the question whether this is also an overstatement of the relevant point. If, as Argyris may imply, all forms of control of others are forms of relationship to be avoided as undesirable, then what sense can we make of the large amount of observations of the cultural anthropologists and of educators as to the actual existence of beneficial controlling forces (e.g., child rearing) in our daily lives in the community, the school and the home? Has not society and the family assigned to the school, in all cultures, the task of "controlling," and even "moulding" the form of self-actualization of the individual? Are they necessarily and invariably productive of "bad" consequences? Or should the "bad" generalization be restricted to a given, specified population-category, e.g., Maslow seems to restrict such an expectation of "good" behavior being produced by acceptance to the "self disciplined and responsible person." (p. 133)

4. Another complex of puzzling questions comes to mind: What are the consequences of autonomous (the "unfolding" of what is latent potentiality within the individual) self-actualization, if the individual could free himself from the press or restrictions of his social milieu (Rousseau's natural man)? Would the results necessarily be the "best" self-actualization (freedom)? Would counseling be needed if the individual, acting alone, is capable of becoming his full humanity? What are the implications for counseling of the concept of authority over or control of others? Is authority equivalent to authoritarianism? Does external authority necessarily debase, thwart, stunt, and corrupt the individual? If unconditional acceptance does "bring out" the best of one's potentiality, does it follow that other techniques of control produce "bad" self-actualization?

5. A fifth puzzling nexus of questions comes to mind as one searches for understanding of the concept of acceptance. If the counselor does not sit in judgment, then is he accepting of the individual's choice of the "best" of his potentiality? What of the many hierarchies of different values in human development? To be sure, Maslow asserts that "peak" experiences (implying an

hierarchy of behavior, rather than an equivalence of all forms of becoming) are real and achievable. But what triggers these peak experiences remains largely unexplained. Are all forms of self-actualization equally, or relatively "good," *if and when self-chosen*, is a relevant question.

Surely no one advocates that we abandon the ancient Greek concept of *arete* (excellence) as irrelevant to the modern age? Yet *arete* is firmly based upon some "external" criteria (i.e., not entirely a self-contained goodness) of the "good" life. Granted that men have long argued about the nature of the "good life" and will likely continue the dialogue into the future, yet does lack of present agreement necessitate turning over to the individual *autonomous* self-determination of his desired form of the "good" life? Is the internal criterion of the "good" life demonstrably more valid, relevant and growth producing than any "external" criteria?

Perhaps the query, "should counselors sit in judgment of students?" is but one more eruption of the age old philosophic search for "criteria" of the good life:—are criteria self-contained within each individual, that is, are there only "internal" criteria; or are there relevant, valid and complementary "external" criteria which "exist" among or "emerge" within the interpersonal experiences and relationships of individual selves; or are there Platonic universals that "exist" apart from individuals' experience and perceptions? Hobbs' contention is relevant: every counselor must perforce "think through" to some kind of personal cosmology. [14] Moreover, one hopes that the counseling relationship will itself aid each counselor to achieve his own personal cosmology.

Could it be that some counselors have not said precisely what they mean by "acceptance" or have not meant precisely what they seem to have said? If this be the case, then surely clarification and precision of concepts, and logic, are much needed to illuminate the peculiar and special way or ways in which the counselor should not sit in judgment of the counselee. Perhaps hasty overgeneralization by some readers has resulted from misinterpretation or overinterpretation of a conviction, held as an operational hypothesis in the counseling relationship, as to effective ways of aiding individuals to seek and, one hopes, to attain the good life. [15]

6. By way of summarizing this effort to examine the concept of acceptance, perhaps it is relevant to recall the *dictum* of the Oracle of Delphi, "nothing in excess!"; perhaps not even "unconditional acceptance?" But the residual query is still with us: *What will* produce "peak" experience, *arete,* or "full" humanity, especially in the case of those whose aspirations presently are less than exhaustive of their full potentiality for humanness?

How can one read the literature of "becoming" one's potentiality (Pindar, daVinci, Concordet, James, Allport, Murphy, Gardner, et al.) without being "moved" by the dynamism of Lenin's admonition "dream forward!" [16] Indeed, I have repeatedly concluded that the counselor must needs be, and indeed is (at his own "peak" experience), an eternal optimist about the outcome of the human enterprise. *But* my hardheaded ancestry "manipulates" me to reiterate Anton Carlson's query (so often quoted by Donald G. Paterson): "*Was ist die* evidence?"

REFERENCES

1. Rogers, C., Toward Becoming a Fully Functioning Person, Chapter 3 in *Perceiving, Behaving, Becoming: A New Focus for Education,* 1962 Yearbook, Washington, D.C.: Association for Supervision and Curriculum Development, p. 22.

   Elsewhere he stated the necessary conditions of the counseling relationship: "an outgoing positive regard for, and acceptance of, the client without reservation, judgment or possessiveness." *On Becoming a Person,* Cambridge, Massachusetts: The Riverside Press, 1961, p. 27.

2. We counselors are often rightly admonished to seek to free ourselves from our middle class value hierarchy, in which "hard work," for example, in the use of our capabilities is elevated to the level of a virtue. An amusing example of this difficult task of freeing is found in the most insightful delineation by Frank Riessman of the problems of educating *The Culturally Deprived Child* (New York: Harper and Brothers, 1962, p. 3). Riessman stresses the necessity of freeing ourselves from our middle class value system concerning odors, dress, cleanliness and polite speech. *But,* he adamantly insists that we *must not yield* to the "anti-intellectual" value hierarchy of these culturally deprived children! Apparently each of us clings to some *sina qua non* value hierachy!

3. Argyris, C., *Interpersonal Competence and Organizational Effectiveness*. Homewood, Illinois: The Dorsey Press, Inc., 1962, p. 18.

4. *Ibid.*

5. Rogers, C. R., The Developing Values of the Growing Person: in *Personality Theory and Counseling Practice*, Papers presented at the First Annual Conference, University of Florida, 1961, p. 27.

6. Maslow, A. H., Psychological Data and Value Theory, in Maslow (Ed.), *New Knowledge in Human Values*. New York: Harper and Brothers, 1959, pp. 131-132.

7. Williamson, E.G., The Societal Responsibilities of Counselors, *Illinois Guidance and Personnel Association Newletter*, Winter, 1963, pp. 5-13.

8. Maslow, A.H., Some Basic Propositions of a Growth and Self-Actualization Psychology, in *Perceiving, Becoming, op. cit.*, Chapter 4, p. 36.

9. Demos, R., Doctors, Philosophers and Teachers. *Harvard Alumni Bulletin,* October 14, 1961.

10. Rogers, C. R., and Skinner, B.F., A Symposium on Some Issues Concerning the Control of Human Behavior. *Science,* November 30, 1956, Vol. 124, pp. 1057-1066.

11. Beck, C.E., *Philosophical Foundations of Guidance*. Englewood Cliffs, New Jersey: Prentice-Hall, Inc., 1963, p. 81.

12. Maslow, *New Knowledge in Human Values, op. cit.*, p. 131.

13. "For him (the modern man) to act as though cruelty were good in itself is no less difficult than to act as though cannibalism were good."
James B. Conant, *Modern Science and Modern Man*. New York: Doubleday and Company, 1953, p. 184.

14. Hobbs, N., Sources of Gain in Psychotherapy. *The American Psychologist,* Vo. 17, No. 11, November 1962, p. 746.

15. In another paper I hope to examine the complicated criteria of the "good life," its many variations. Elsewhere I have argued that in the counseling relationship the essential utility of the counselor is to aid the student to perceive and examine, thoughtfully, the many options open to his consideration for adoption as his own guidelines of self development of potentiality. My position is related to Muller's concept of freedom as: "free, rational consent (choice), in an awareness of alternatives." (Muller, H.J., *Issues of Freedom*. New York: Harper and Brothers, 1960, p. 155.)

While the individual possesses the moral right (and moral duty) to the choice of his form of the "good" life, we educator-counselors serve as "teachers" to introduce the student to thoughtful consideration and evaluation of the consequences and advantages of each of the several optional forms of the "good" life, that is, to the many value hierarchies available for adoption as guiding principles, external criteria, of human existence.

16. Steiner, G., On Paul Goodman. *Commentary*, Vol. 36, No. 2, August 1963, p. 160.

THE SCHOOL AND THE SOCIAL SYSTEM

GORDON KLOPF

Associate Professor of Education
Bank Street College of Education

Dr. Klopf delineates the influences of the social sciences on guidance. He shows how the economic and social events in the recent past have left their mark on educational programs. The fact that specialization will mark the life of the future will also influence the educator and the counselor. He recalls Horney's contention that society's values are at times contradictory and they thus produce conflict in the young. The cultural background of students may also foster conflict as students face the expectations of another culture during schooling. Kluckholm's four "determinants" of personality and the findings of Coleman concerning the adolescent society are reviewed. He concludes that while the social background of the school should be studied, the educator must keep his ideals high and regard the present situation as an "avenue of opportunity."

In *Society, Its Structure and Change* [1] Robert MacIver has said that to understand things is to perceive their connectedness and thus their relations to some whole to which they all belong. Today in talking about guidance, I am going to begin by making some observations about the whole, the larger society, in which our schools are working and functioning and in which our students are going to live and in which they and their parents are now living. We have to look at guidance in relationship to the larger whole.

Recent Social Upheavals

Someone has said that the modern teacher will only succeed if he is capable of seeing each of the problems of the new generation against the background of a changing world. I think those of us working in guidance have to see the economic, cultural and social development of our country. Those of you who lived in the Thirties know that there were several economic and social problems. It was a time of real social concern on the part of people, unemployment, youth projects like CCC and NYA. Some of the means by which we now deal with social and economic issues and needs were developed during these years.

In the early Forties we· saw the war, the great scarcity of manpower and in the late Forties the veterans coming to higher education with the accompanying expansion in these institutions. The Fifties brought different developments. Each period has seen its economic and social impact in determining the role guidance plays.

The Future: Some Educational Issues

What does the future hold? Great specialization and less need for unskilled labor. But with this specialization comes the need for flexibility, with a readiness for retraining. The girl who took typing ten years ago or seven years ago, and who can't use an electric typewriter with ease and skill, perhaps would have difficulty holding a job or getting a position today in New York City. Our changing society creates certain issues in the field of education.

One of these issues is "hard" versus "soft" education, which has developed somewhat as a result of our competition with Russia. And this is a real conflict. Should education be hard? Are we only concerned with the academic? Should we try to deal with the person as a human being and look at the whole student? Actually it is not one or the other. Effective education involves knowledge and content but deals with the learner in terms of his background and needs.

Integration is a very key issue for education and has real implications for guidance counselors. Several years ago in a Mid-Western city guidance counselors were telling Negro students they should not choose professions because there would be no employment opportunity. They would not be admitted to professional schools and the professions themselves. The guidance counselors were not very daring, imaginative or right, as they counseled with these young people. There have however, been a number of recent projects in the same city to change some of these approaches of counselors with Negro students.

There is the issue of the selection process in education. To what degree are we going to become like England where children are selected at a very early age for certain channels in education? The students cannot change later because they are in a vocational or technical education program. The tests they took at ten or eleven years of age set the course of their life. Tests serve a real purpose, but they should only be one factor in the decision making process.

Values and Society

The values of society today create certain conflicts. Karen Horney [2] summarizes the three basic conflicts in the values of our culture today. The first conflict, she says is "that between competition and success on the one hand, and brotherly love and humility on the other." We teach in our churches and schools the concept of brotherhood, the idea of learning to live and share with one another. Yet to succeed in the same school where we teach brotherhood we say you have to get the A to get the gold medal, to have your teachers like you, you have to compete. We expect aggressiveness, we want competitiveness, we want the child to achieve, to struggle for survival. The child is really lost between the discussion of brotherhood, of "doing unto others as you would have them do unto you" and the real life situations. But on the other hand, we want the individual to do better than the other does.

A second conflict which Horney mentions is that "between the stimulation of our needs and our factual frustrations in satisfying them." Recent studies on youth describe this age group as wanting paraphanalia, transistor radios, portable record players, cars, and clothes. The conflict regarding material things does not exist among the middle class youths but among the children of the lower socio-economic group. These young people see the material things which other youths have and enjoy. They too want them badly but they do not have them and their parents cannot furnish them. And this urgently felt need may lead them to conflict and to trouble. Some authorities believe that many problems of young people in the lower socio-economic group are due to this desire for "the things" of life.

The last conflict Horney mentions is that "between the alleged freedom of the individual and his factual limitations." We stress the opportunities that freedom gives youth, but in many areas such as choosing occupations and recreation the actual possibilities are limited. We forget to help youth to realize that in a given culture the notion of necessary controls parallels that of freedom, and that along with freedom goes responsibility. We constantly talk about the rights of citizens, the rights of people, but we forget to discuss that freedom does not mean license, that it means that there are controls, and that we are responsible for the things we do.

Rollo May[3] also emphasizes the importance of responsibility. He says that we who are working with the youth today may have failed to help young people to accept responsibility for their own actions and their own activities. However, think of the child who is living in the Harlem slums. His range of choice, due to a very different background and exposure, is not broad and we cannot say how responsible he is for all he does. He is not aware of all of the choices. For him they are not there; they may be in the larger world, but they may have no meaning for him and he may not know they exist.

Culture and Testing

To help us understand the larger society we need to look to a greater degree, to the work of the anthropologist, the social psychologist, and the sociologist. Some of our new guidance testbooks, like Miller's *Foundations of Guidance,*[4] gives emphasis to this approach. What have these disciplines brought to the field of guidance? First of all, I think they have made us conscious of the concept of culture and the importance of culture in relationship to our functions and techniques, such as, tests and counseling. One of the leaders in the measurement field reports a very simple little story illustrating the effect of culture on tests. He tells of his own three-year-old child who took a very simple intelligence test and was asked by the psy-

chometrist, "Do fish swim or jump?" Now he says it so happened
that this little boy had a fish that jumped. In his room he had a
fish bowl with fish who jumped. These were the fish he knew. So
he told the psychometrist, "fish jumped." In his culture, in his
environment, fish jumped, and he failed in this response. Tests
measure what you know at the hour of your life when you are
taking that test. They measure the culture and environment
in which you have grown and developed. Now we have had
a good deal of work in the past ten years led by Allison Davis
on the development of culture free tests. The people who are
the critics of these attempts to develop culture free tests say that
it's unreal for students to take a culture free test. The student
who is going to go to Fordham University, Columbia or to
Rosary Hill College, where the learning is based on the middle
class culture, is going to have to know the words that you need
to succeed at Fordham, Columbia, or Rosary Hill. Most of
these are middle class, urban, intellectually oriented words. If
he does not have the basic intellectual aptitude measured by
tests we are uncertain about his potential for survival in college.
As we work with young people, we have to be very sensitive
to the fact that "rights" and "wrongs" in values, mores, and
behavior are frequently culturally oriented. When the young
person comes into our setting, he must understand our expectations of him and what we, in our particular setting, consider
right and wrong.

Social Class and Education

Another very important factor that the sociologist has made
us aware of is the concept of class. We know that class is a real
determinant of who goes to school and what school you go to.
There is a positive relationship of class to educational opportunity. Some authorities believe also that the factor of class is the
most important determinant in the opportunities one has and
the direction one takes.

"Determinants" of Personality

We usually study personality from the standpoint or view
of the psychologist. However, the cultural anthropologist has

made us aware of the relationship of personality to culture. Kluckholm, [5] an outstanding cultural anthropologist, says that there are four basic determinants of what a person is. I would like to review them because I think they are important for the counselor and the guidance worker.

The first determinant of what we are as a person, Kluckholm says, is the constitutional factor, that which we inherit, the genetic potential of a person. But no matter what the person's genetic potential is, it takes certain life situations that bring it out. The child in Harlem may not have the life situations that bring out the best of his genetic potential. So it is not just the genetic potential which is a determinant of what you are; it is also what we call the life opportunity.

A second factor is group membership, the group into which you are born. That group which you are born into and move into, is a real determinant of how you live and how you behave, and what you say and what you do.

A third factor is that of role. You might call it the culti- vated surface. People behave in certain ways because these are the role expectations. You behave in certain ways because of the expectations people, groups, society and tradition have of you.

Now the fourth determinant Kluckholm points out is that of the situation or chance. And this to me is always the most interesting. One of the four reasons why you are what you are, is chance. You may be on a train seated next to someone, talk- ing to them about a job, about education, you take this lead and follow it and it changes your whole life. Chance might be a much greater factor in life than some of the guidance counsel- ing we do.

The Class and the School as Social System

The behavioral scientist has helped us to look at education and at the individual as living not only in society, in a culture and in a class, but to look at each school and each classroom itself as a social system. Professional workers in elementary schools find that the school itself does not have the impact upon the child, the whole school, as much as does the high school or the college. To the child the social system, the social

3. *High School Counselor*

community, the unit to which he is attached, is the classroom. The teacher is very important to the child and his society is the class.

As the child gets older and goes into the junior and senior high schools, the whole school becomes his social system. An early study of the social system of the secondary school has been done by James Coleman. Everyone in secondary education should have read his *Adolescent Society*. [6] He studied in public and parochial schools in the greater Chicago area and found that the subcultural group, the cliques in the school, have a stronger impact as a learning force than the teacher, the books, or many of the formal instructional media of the school. It is interesting that of the ten schools he studied in Chicago, the one that had the best milieu for learning was a boys' parochial high school which had the poorest facilities of the ten schools. It was a school in which the boys came from all over the city of Chicago. They came without neighborhood cliques, had no pre-established friendships. The school had a good deal of emphasis on learning. There were rewards for learning as well as for athletic and activity achievement. Now in the suburban school which had excellent facilities, the emphasis was less on learning and less learning took place. It had better facilities, and in some ways better trained teachers. But it had a whole network of gangs and leadership cliques. The students followed the social goals of the cliques and groups. The group was the chief determinant of what they did and its goals and activities were not necessarily learning oriented.

The concept of reward in these schools is an interesting one. Coleman says, and this we all know is true, the people who have the best awards for the adolescents are the athletic coaches. And what do we do for academic honors? We give them a tea, or have a very uninteresting assembly. And what do the coaches do? They give blankets, big letters, cups, medals and pins, and jackets, all the things which are important to the adolescent. The coaches who perhaps have the least problem of motivation have the most effective reward system.

Looking at the college as the social system we have the recent work in the past four or five years of Pace and Stern. Pace and Stern [7] are psychologists who developed a set of questions for examining the characteristics of a college, such as, what expectations a college has of its students. And they have a set of questions to find out what the students' needs are. Their devices are also being used to examine the social system of the high school and college.

These are helpful devices but the real issue is how are they to be used. Do high school counselors and college advisers analyze colleges and students and send the student to the college whose environment best meets the student's needs? We need to give the student the optimal atmosphere for living. This does not always mean the environment which appears to be most agreeable to that student. He may need some challenge. Perhaps he should be in an environment where he will not live as he has always lived or where he will do the things he has always been doing.

Importance of Leadership

It has been said that institutions are deliberately designed environments. A principal in a secondary school has a tremendous impact on that school. I have known a high school in the state of Montana, a culturally deprived area if there ever was one. The children all come from a low socio-economic group. The principal brings teachers to that school with a good deal of academic orientation and the children in this school have as rich a cultural opportunity in the wilds of Montana as they do in some of our fine suburban areas around New York City. The principal has a conviction that an educational environment must be the best possible even in the bareness of a rural plain. He hires teachers who have rich backgrounds and respect his goals for the school. The children have excellent learning experience in spite of the limitations of their family and location.

In conclusion, I think that we must realize that the guidance counselor, the dean of students, the principal, and the teacher, all have tremendous impact on youth. The school and its society should be an avenue of opportunity and we as counselors should help make it such.

REFERENCES

1. MacIver, R. M. *Society, Its Structure and Change.* New York: R. Long and R. R. Smith, 1931.
2. Horney, Karen *The Neurotic Personality of Our Time. New York:* W. W. Norton, 1937.
3. May, R. *Man's Search for Himself.* New York: W. W. Norton, 1953.
4. Miller, C. H. *Foundations of Guidance.* New York: Harper and Row, 1961.
5. Kluckholm, C. and Murray, H. A. *Personality in Nature, Society and Culture.* (2nd ed.) New York: A. Knopf, 1953.
6. Coleman, J. *The Adolescent Society.* Glencove, Ill.: The Free Press, 1961.
7. Pace, R. C. and Stern, G. G. *A Criterion Study of College Environment.* Syracuse, N. Y.: Syracuse University Psychological Research Center, 1958.

RATIONAL AND IRRATIONAL CRITICISM
OF THE GUIDANCE MOVEMENT

ANTHONY C. RICCIO

Associate Professor of Education
The Ohio State University

To offer an overview of the current guidance scene, Dr. Riccio examines certain charges which come from responsible sources that guidance aims towards excessive conformity on the part of our youth, that testing penalizes the outstanding student and that guidance personnel are unrealistic in evaluating their role. In addition, he illustrates other charges from what he regards as irresponsible sources. In view of these criticisms, he recommends improvement in the communication between the home and the school regarding the tasks of guidance, and urges that guidance workers study carefully the criticism which is made of their work. Of some criticism he notes that "the positive changes they suggest we might well heed." But there are other cases when "we must engage these critics in public debate and expose them."

The Guidance Movement has never received a more favorable press than it has received in the last five years. Accolades have come from Congressional groups, from James B. Conant—and even from Admiral Hyman Rickover. Although these groups and people have seldom shared the conceptualization of guidance services posited by professionals, they have nevertheless been instrumental in selling guidance to the public. Guidance has never had it so good.

There is developing, however, a growing number of opponents to guidance and other psychological services. Some of the critics are sincere in their criticisms; they raise some cogent questions which merit thoughtful answers. A larger group of critics, however, appears to be obsessed with relating guidance to un-American activity—indeed, some have gone so far as to view guidance as a major component of the Communist conspiracy.

As Schlessinger [1] has noted, lunatic fringe groups in society are not posing a major threat nationally. They are, nevertheless, a fearsome force in the lives of school counselors and other professional personnel in many local communities. In fact, the number of communities in which guidance services, especially psychological testing, have come under attack has become so large that the Resolutions Committee of the American Personnel and Guidance Association felt impelled to present the following resolution to the APGA Senate at the Boston Convention:

> Whereas the use of educational and psychological tests in our culture is currently under criticism, and whereas the professional use of such instruments continues to constitute an important part of counseling and guidance, BE IT RESOLVED that the American Personnel and Guidance Association, through its National Office and its various Divisions, reaffirms its commitment to the professional and ethical use of such tests, and to the professional safeguards against the development and use of improper tests. [2]

This resolution was adopted by an overwhelming majority, but the fact that it was necessary to present such a resolution is indicative of the growing opposition to guidance services.

PURPOSE

It is the purpose of this paper to identify and discuss some of the current criticisms of guidance. The criticisms will be discussed in terms of the sources from which they emanate. For this purpose, I have established two basic categories: (1) those criticisms which are leveled by individuals and groups who appear to be friends of education and are truly interested in working for better schools; (2) those criticisms which emanate from individuals or groups which appear to be critical of a great many facets of our society and who are generally regarded as critical primarily of economic and political postures in America.

I am ready and willing to admit that any such classification is subjective and judgmental in nature. But these are times when individuals must stand up and be counted.

RESPONSIBLE CRITICISMS

The "Maladjusted," "Conformity," and Society

1. It is a pet thesis of many commentators on the social scene that all significant progress in society comes about as the result of the efforts of people who would be categorized as maladjusted by professional educators—or in a broader sense, as undesirables. There is ample evidence to support this thesis. One has but to think of the difficulties of the Puritans and the Mormons as well as a host of other beleaguered groups who—continually attacked by the larger segments of society—found their way to new and strange lands and established what are today thriving metropolitan areas. Some individuals in this nation who have made the great strides in medicine and science possible are not generally people whom we would normally consider well-adjusted; they are people who had dreams and who were obsessed with the desire to achieve certain objectives—no matter what the cost to themselves and their loved ones. They were people with a cause; they were driven. They were not well-adjusted. They did things because they wanted to do them; because they had to do them. They were not "other-directed" people.

A number of people in our educational institutions—generally professors of the liberal disciplines—are critical of guidance and counseling services because they feel that we have "built an industry out of guidance of the young." It has been charged that we in guidance have joined in the campaign to make people "more and more alike . . . in the bedrock of conceptions we have of life: what it is all about, what we are in the world for, and what we are supposed to be doing with our precious three-score and ten." [3]

It is ironic that guidance, an activity so heavily grounded in differential psychology, should be accused of fostering conformity and of squelching productive idiosyncrasy. But the truth of the matter is that the average school counselor comes into contact with very few eccentric geniuses who are going to set the world on fire; he does come into contact with scores of average students who are in need of information so that they can make adequate choices in the problems that confront them. There is little doubt about the fact that school counselors *are* concerned about the decisions that counselees make. They generally have pretty distinct notions of the alternative solutions to conflicts that they wish to see chosen by counselees. There is no doubt that counselors oftentimes, unconsciously perhaps, force choices upon counselees. Let us never forget that the counselor is an agent of socialization, and that each agent of socialization teaches the way of life that he values. [4] It is true, as Morris charges, that most counselors would discourage a bright high-school graduate from riding a bicycle around the world in preference to attending college. [5] It is also true, as Morris claims further, that few counselors have gone around the world on a bike and are fully cognizant of the educational and personal advantages of such an excursion. [6] But does not the counselor have an obligation to present to the youth with whom he comes into contact the probable consequences of his choices? Should the counselor encourage all who come to him to do what at first blush they indicate they would like to do? Is not counseling more than encouragement? I think it is. Counseling, to my way of thinking, is an attempt to assist counselees to develop the virtue of appropriate decision-making. It is really an application of the virtue of prudence to the problems of daily living. There is no inconsistency in helping a youth discover that most of our decisions have consequences in the social order, but that there are times when our root beliefs demand that we make decisions which have negative social consequences—decisions which force us to stand up and be counted.

It is important that we help counselees to learn the roles expected of them in our society; it is equally important that we help them to realize that there are times when they must rise up in righteous indignation against roles that are being pressed upon them. We are not interested in fostering non-conformity for the sake of non-conformity—but non-conformity with a purpose is another matter.

Furore Over Testing

2. Related to the first criticism of guidance discussed above is the criticism that the kinds of objective tests employed in guidance—and actions predicated upon these test scores—discriminate against brilliant students in favor of mediocre students. Banesh Hoffman, in an article in *Harper's* in 1961 [7] and more recently in his book on *The Tyranny of Testing* [8], has made this charge. Hoffman has taken several items from very well-known tests and has attempted to show that a brilliant student could see the logical answer in more than one of the distractors—and conceivably make an incorrect response in terms of the keys; whereas a mediocre student with a limited or superficial knowledge of the subject of the item would have no difficulty in answering the item correctly. There is little doubt that this kind of criticism has some merit; we hate to see an individual penalized for being exceedingly well-informed.

But what Hoffman fails to appreciate is that the objective test comprised of several hundred items is a much fairer instrument than a one or two question essay-type examination—a test in which the problem of reader bias becomes strong. A brilliant student's score on a lengthy multiple-choice examination is not likely to be hurt appreciably because of two items which have more than one "correct" answer.

Among the factors responsible for the growing interest in testing in this country are the growing demand for college education and the increasing complexity of our society which demands that—in the interest of conserving human energy and financial resources—men be placed on jobs in which they can become productive as soon as possible. [9] Testing is playing a very important role these days in both college admissions and job placement. This factor has proved very threatening to many people. As John Gardner has noted in his book *Excellence*:

> It must never be forgotten that a person born to low status in a rigidly stratified society has a far more acceptable self-image than the person who loses out in our free competition of talent. In an older society, the humble member of society can attribute his lowly status to God's will, to the ancient order of things or to a corrupt and tyrannous government. But if a society sorts people

out efficiently and fairly according to their gifts, the loser knows that the true reason for his lowly status is that he is not capable of better. That is a bitter pill for any man. [10]

People will continue to criticize our tests, and we must try to make them better. But until the critics come up with solutions that are better than the things that we are currently doing, we must simply tolerate their criticisms as containing a certain amount of validity. We must realize that the criticism is in large measure symptomatic of the anxiety that people undergo when college selection is based on test performance rather than financial resources and parental prestige.

Confusion Over the Role of the Counselor

3. Another criticism which is being made of guidance relates to the self-images of guidance workers as they are perceived by others. In general, the criticism is made by teachers, administrators, and other professional personnel that guidance workers view themselves as chosen people. I personally believe there is some merit to this criticism—and I think I can understand how a good many counselors do perceive themselves to be a notch above the average worker in our school system.

We must remember that guidance has enjoyed a fantastic growth in the last five years. In 1959 there were 7000 counselors in our public schools; in 1962 there were almost 16,000 counselors. The National Defense Education Act of 1958 had much to do with this increase in the number of counselors—as did the Conant Report and recommendations of the North Central Association of Colleges and Secondary Schools. The NDEA Training Institutes and its attractive financial aspects lured many people—sincere and otherwise—to apply for admission. There were so many more applicants than there were places that the institute directors had incredible selection problems. Many applied, but few were chosen. The intensive nature of the institute experiences lead many enrollees to conclude that survival through such rigorous experiences did indeed make them a special kind of person. (Parenthetically, it should be noted that not all who were chosen survived. Casualties ranged from suicide to mental breakdowns to voluntary removal from the program.)

Many of the institute programs were also interdisciplinary in nature. Institute participants frequently acquired insights and value patterns which were not shared by other members of the school staff. They were different from others in the school setting. They even had difficulty in communicating with their peers. Further, a number of counselors have gained in their preparation programs a hostility toward school administrators, who, not having had intensive formal training in guidance, did not appreciate the contributions that counselors could make to the school program. In a number of cases, the role expectancies that counselors have set for themselves are not shared by those exercising influence in their school setting.

Several comments are here in order with respect to the relationships that frequently obtain between the guidance worker and the classroom teacher. Personal experience has lead me to believe that most teachers are convinced that physical education teachers and guidance workers have the easiest jobs in the school setting. At least, no group of teachers takes more ribbing or needling than these two groups. Unless the guidance worker defends himself, what started out as jest may come to be regarded as objective facts. The guidance worker owes it to himself and to his profession to dispel the notion that guidance is a soft touch. As Toops has noted in a mimeographed report entitled "Seventy-Five Ways to Become a Genius:" "Toot your own horn; people are more than willing to accept your evaluation of yourself." [11]

Because of a mistaken notion of the meaning of confidentiality in the guidance interview, guidance workers sometimes unwittingly antagonize many classroom teachers. They expect teachers to refer students to them, but they do not inform teachers of the outcome of interviews, believing teachers to be too unsophisticated to handle the elicited information or believing that such information is to be regarded as sacrosanct. They fail to distinguish between information gained from a student who has been referred by a teacher and that information gained from a self-referred student.

An Illustration of the Uncertainty

In a Principles of Guidance course I recently taught, I employed a technique that demonstrates vividly what classroom teachers expect from guidance counselors to whom they have referred students. Prior to the introduction of a unit on the role of the classroom teacher in the guidance program, students were asked to complete, anonymously, the statement: "If I referred a student to a counselor, . . . " This technique was employed to provide the instructor with an opportunity in the next class to generate a discussion in which the class, to some extent, would be ego-involved. The thirty-three students who responded to the statement were all classroom teachers, and none had had a previous course in guidance.

The responses of students were sorted and categorized in terms of statements that were typical of a number of responses. Since some of the students completed the statement by constructing a compound-complex sentence, there was a total of forty-one responses made by the thirty-three students. The most frequent responses were the following:

1. Seventeen, or forty-one percent of the responses, indicated that if teachers referred a student to counselors, they would expect the counselors to give them a report on the matter so that they might be aided in working with the students in the future.
2. Seven, or seventeen per cent of the responses, indicated that if teachers referred a student to counselors, they would give the counselors what information they had on the student.
3. Another seventeen per cent indicated that teachers referred students because they could not cope with the problem at hand.

These responses demonstrate that teachers are willing to cooperate with counselors, but they expect to be informed of the results of the ensuing activity. The information that counselors give teachers should be couched in meaningful language and should be pertinent to what the teacher can do to improve the particular situation. The amount of information that the counselor gives the teacher should be influenced by the counselor's knowledge of the moral fibre of the teacher involved. Browning has noted, pertinent to using the information we gain through guidance services, that

> we can assume that professional persons are like all other human beings; they will *tend* to enhance their own status by using other people. They don't want consciously to hurt those whom they use, but they can't help it. This is their finite dilemma. Therefore, they will be a little unethical here and there—in the sense that the stature of others will be somewhat downgraded and they will be somewhat upgraded. What I am saying is this: I do not think it possible to gather the information gathered in interviews without some *injustice* to the student involved. [12]

This fact, however, is not a sufficient reason for the veto of the process. We would make so many more mistakes without the information than with it that we must, by all means, continue to gather and keep it and try to use it well. At the same time, we must attempt to keep to a minimum the damage that can be done by people who, in Robinson's terms, love to "glory in the gory." [13]

Importance of Communication with Teachers

In order to work effectively with teachers, it is necessary for the guidance worker to know the perceptions of guidance services held by the teachers in his school. No program of guidance services can be effective if members of the teaching staff lack a proper understanding of the contributions that guidance can legitimately claim to make the realization of school objectives. This point is exceedingly important for more often than not teachers have a tendency to view guidance services as remedial and preventive in nature rather than as developmental. This factor will account for the kinds of students that teachers will refer to the counselor and will also, consciously or not, play no small part in the opinions that teachers will hold of the effectiveness of the guidance program. If, for example, the teacher believes that guidance services are primarily remedial in nature, he will refer nothing but behavior problems to the guidance counselor. He will never think of referring intelligent, high-achieving students to the counselor, so that partially as a result of counseling these students might perform at new levels

of academic excellence. The classroom teacher who has a concept of guidance as a remedial service will probably not regard
the counseling interview as a learning situation, and, in all probability, will not realize that like all other learning situations, the
more intelligent the student the greater the probability that he
will profit from the learning experience. There can be no doubt
about it: one of the major tasks of the guidance worker is to
make clear to teachers what guidance *is* and what it can do for
the school community.

IRRESPONSIBLE CRITICISMS

The criticisms discussed above have generally emanated
from people who are truly interested in helping the school
achieve its objectives. But guidance services are also under
attack from people and groups whom Raywid has labeled "ax-
grinder." [14] These in most cases are individuals and groups cut
across political and religious lines. Their numbers include
Democrats, Republicans, and State-Righters, Catholics, and non-
Catholics. The media in which their charges appear range from
scurrilous unsigned materials to *The Homiletic and Pastoral
Review.* [15]

The charges leveled at guidance by these groups may fall
into one or more of the following categories: (a) charges based
on complete misinformation, (b) charges based on inferences
drawn from only part of the facts, and (c) emotionally-charged
opinions.

Guidance as Instrument of Federal Control

1. A number of extreme right-wing groups are upset at guidance
services simply because there is Federal support available to
improve guidance in our schools. The January 1962 issue of the
Bulletin of the National Health Federation is a special issue on
school counseling. [16] The editor of this issue notes that with
funds emanating from the U.S. Office of Education counselors
are "to be given from six months to one year of training, to the
end that they may know what is expected of them. The counse-

lors are to ride herd on the teachers and to evaluate both the teacher and the children, based on the answers to all types of questions.

"Not only will it be the duty of these counselors to evaluate the children and the teachers, but also the parents and the homes of the children.

" . . . this (is a) move of the Federal government to control the minds of the nation's children." [17]

Means of Brainwashing

2. A number of right-wingers have attacked such instruments as the SRA (Science Research Associates) Youth Inventory and the Mooney Problem Check List. They have gone so far as to suggest non-existent items are being administered to our youth, and further, that these non-existent items are possibly part of a Communist conspiracy to brainwash American youth.

One Columbus newscaster stated on November 15, 1961, that a "Worthington (a suburb of Columbus, Ohio) man phoned this reporter today to say that he understood that one of the questions being given students on this type of test is: 'Would you rather spit on the Bible, or your best friend?' A Catholic parent said that he understood that in the parochial school test of this nature, which to the best of this reporter's knowledge has not been given here, the question is changed to read: 'Would you rather spit on the Crucifix or on your best friend?' "

Unfamiliar with such items and unwilling to believe that any school counselor would be so stupid as to engage in such activity, I challenged this reporter in public debate to name the instruments in which these items were found or to name the schools in which they were administered. He could come up with no answers, but this failure to check sources in no way embarrassed him. He is still campaigning against guidance services by employing such tactics.

Confusion over Specialties and Instruments

3. In a recent television debate [18] I had with Congressman John Ashbrook of Ohio, I was appalled to note how difficult

it was to communicate to him the simple concepts that I introduce to first-year students in guidance. Mr. Ashbrook, for example, equates the administration of the SRA Youth Inventory with psychoanalysis—and concluded that school counselors are not equipped to do psychoanalysis (a conclusion I share with him.) It is impossible to convince him that there is a world of difference between the simple administration of a low-level problem checklist and the long term process of depth analysis.

It should also be noted that attacks have not been made against problem checklists alone. Such reputable achievement tests as the *Iowa Tests of Educational Development* and the *Sequential Tests of Educational Progress* have also been attacked as Communist-inspired instruments, because in reading passages social and economic issues are discussed.

Not even cumulative records have been spared. Josephine Hindman, in an article appearing in the *American Mercury* entitled "Secret Cum Files; A Leftist Wedge," describes cumulative records as a plot to separate children from their parents by having them committed to schools and classes for the mentally retarded. [20]

It should be clear by this time that guidance is indeed under attack from a number of quarters. It should be equally clear that it is impossible to deal with people who believe that Communism is a synonym for the income tax, federal aid to education, collective bargaining, and all social legislation that depends in whole or in part on public revenues. Such critics are not men of good will. They are not interested in informing themselves on the topics in question. They are unwilling to face up to the complexity of our modern world. Everything, for them, is red or blue—and they alone are qualified to call the colors. But—thank heavens—the vast majority of Americans are not left-wing or right-wing extremists. Most Americans are willing to examine evidence before arriving at conclusions. And it is this large majority of Americans to whom guidance workers must bring their case.

RECOMMENDATIONS

I would like to conclude my comments with three recommendations that guidance workers should follow if they are to meet successfully the rising tide of criticisms against guidance services.

1. Guidance workers should forestall further attacks on guidance programs by the establishment of a thorough system of communication between the school and the home. A thorough explanation of the guidance program and of any innovations in established procedure can go far toward preventing attacks, whether spontaneous or incited, that might occur when the local citizens are not well informed about their schools. The public has a right and a newly emergent desire to know what the schools are trying to do, how well they are succeeding, and whether or not they are doing what is best for the pupils. We must be able to give parents complete and accurate answers, for if we do not they will be susceptible to the distortions of the ax-grinders in our communities.

2. Guidance workers and other school personnel should become familiar with responsible material concerning the critics of the guidance movement. If we are to combat the critics of guidance, we must understand them in terms of their fears and insecurities, their motivations and objectives. We can never underestimate the importance of being well informed about people who are critical of our profession and the work we are doing.

3. Finally, we must listen to our critics to determine whether we can learn anything from them. The positive changes they suggest we might well heed; but when we believe that the critics are up to no good, when we believe that the critics are attempting to use the school in general and some of our school programs in particular to achieve political or economic aims—we must engage these critics in public debate and expose them for what they are. For the day is long past when professional educators can naively remain free of the political arena.

REFERENCES

1. Schlessinger, A. Jr. The Threat of the Radical Right. *New York Times Magazine* (June 17, 1962), 10 ff.
2. Resolutions Committee, American Personnel and Guidance Association, Boston, April 9, 1963, dittoed.

3. Morris, V.C. Conformity, Rebellion, and the Authentic Life: a Look at Contemporary Guidance Theory. *Teachers College Record,* 61 (October, 1959), 46-50.

4. See Ricco, A. C. Does Guidance Need A Philosophy? *The School Counselor,* 10 (December, 1962), 58-59.

5. Morris, *op. cit.*

6. *Ibid.*

7. Hoffman, B. The Tyranny of Multiple-Choice Tests. *Harper's Magazine,* 222 (March, 1961), 37-41.

8. Hoffman B. *The Tyranny of Testing.* New York: Harper and Bros., 1962.

9. Goslin, D. A. *The Search for Ability: Standardized Testing in Social Perspective.* New York: Russell Sage Foundation, 1963.

10. Gardner, J. W. *Excellence.* New York: Harper and Bros., 1961, 71-72.

11. Toops, H. A. Seventy-Five Ways to Become a Genius. Columbus: The Ohio State University, 1956. p. 2. mimeographed.

12. Browning, R. Ethical Considerations In Handling Information Gained through the Inventory Service. Columbus: The Ohio State University, 1956, mimeographed.

13. Robinson, F. P. *Principles and Procedures in Student Counseling.* New York: Harper and Bros., 1950.

14. Raywid, M. A. *The Ax-Grinders.* New York: Macmillan, 1962.

15. Noonan J. E. Disturbance through Guidance. *Homiletic and Pastoral Review* (July, 1959).

16. *National Health Federation Bulletin* (School Counselor Edition), VIII (January, 1962).

17. *Ibid.,* pp. 3-4.

18. Viewpoint. Coumbus, Ohio, WLWC Television Channel, November 19, 1962.

19. See Buford, C.D. Jr., A Critical Analysis of Selected Criticisms of the Guidance Movement. Unpublished Master's thesis, The Ohio State University, 1962, 74-79.

20. Hindman, Jo, Secret Cum Files: A Leftist Wedge. *American Murcury* (October, 1958) 118-126.

Part II:
PRACTICAL

PROGRAM DEVELOPMENT OF GUIDANCE IN A LARGE URBAN SETTING

NATHAN BROWN

Assistant Superintendent, Division of Child Welfare,
Pupil Personnel Services, New York City

Dr. Brown describes the guidance activities and problems in each of the three levels of schools under his direction. In the elementary school there is the Early Identification and Prevention Program, the Play Group Program and Junior Guidance. The work of guidance in the junior high school is primarily the choice of occupation and senior high school, but there is also an important "career guidance" program. The senior high schools and their special problems are also considered. Guidance services for the maladjusted and handicapped are described. An excellent summary of the Higher Horizons and related programs is given. Problems which the working counselor and his supervisor faces are suggested for dicussion.

I am going to discuss the program developed for guidance and counseling in a large urban center. However, the basic difference between the guidance programs in large and small school systems is quantitative. Whereas we might have specialists dealing with certain aspects of a guidance program, in a small school district the same person might do three or four of the same things we are discussing. I believe that in every community there is a need for some aspect of the program which I am going to describe.

My plan in this paper is to propose certain conditions pertaining to philosophy and the individuals involved which influence the guidance program. Then I will offer a brief sketch of the almost myriad activities which involve guidance at all levels in

a large urban center. Finally, I will suggest for your consideration what I believe are some basic issues or problems which
confront the guidance staff in the large urban center.

LOCAL CONDITIONS

Philosophy of the School

The guidance worker is always influenced to a great degree
by the conditions which exist in his school system. Here the
primary consideration is the overall philosophy of the school
system. Is it committed to particular values? Is it consistently
searching for additional knowledge? Does it have a stand,
expressed or implied, on the meaning and equality of man? These
and many other questions pertaining to deeper problems of life
must be answered and programs consistent with the answers
must be developed, or else problems of vacillation and confusion
will plague the system. Let us take an example. In New York
City, we are all concerned with the problem of integration. The
guidance program which is based on integration as the objective
is going to be quite different from the program which would be
required if the objective is limited to equality of education for all.

Background of the Children

A second factor which conditions the guidance program
is obviously the type of child in the district. The needs of the
child in the primarily agricultural area will differ in many ways
from the needs of the child in the suburbs or in the central part
of the city. By way of illustration, in New York City we have
a large number of children who come before the courts. It is
therefore imperative that our guidance program include a staff
to work with the courts on behalf of these children. Furthermore,
we have a number of children who have been returned from
custodial and mental institutions. Our guidance program must
also provide for staff members to be concerned with these
children. Of course, these children constitute but a small percentage of the children with whom our guidance program works,

but a consideration of these atypical children strengthens my contention that guidance programs are influenced by the needs of the children in the area.

Adequately Trained Staff

The availability of adequate staff is another important factor which conditions a guidance program. If it were to be decided tomorrow that all of the guidance programs in the senior high schools in New York City must be staffed by full time professionally trained counselors there would be considerable difficulty in complying. Of course, the problem of obtaining professionally trained counselors is not merely local but is nationwide. In many districts a full time guidance program has not been initiated largely because of the difficulty of obtaining trained counselors. In New York City we recognize that not all of the thousand people who are doing guidance work in the senior high schools have the 30 graduate credits required for certification. However, we are moving gradually towards the goal of using the services of only professionally trained counselors.

Relationship Between Pupil Personnel Services

Another factor that influences the guidance program is the local relationship between the guidance services and other pupil personnel services. Some school systems, particularly in suburban areas around New York, Chicago and Philadelphia, have a school psychological service. Such a service very often combines the guidance program that we have in the New York City elementary schools, on which I shall elaborate later, with the testing and measurement function; such a service is not clinically oriented. This orientation, in effect, conditions the guidance program in those school systems. In other communities, such as New York City, the school-based counselor has a specified relationship to other members of the pupil personnel team: the clinical psychologist, the attendance teacher, the school social worker, and the speech teacher, most of whom do not serve in a specific school on a full-time basis; in this type of program the psychiatrist is a clinical consultant for the mental health team. Clearly, the work of the guidance staff will be influenced by the presence or absence in the program of these specialized workers.

Approach to Guidance

Earlier the importance of the philosophy of the school system was indicated. The importance of the philosophy of the guidance program also must be appreciated as very influential in this scene. Many areas of the guidance program will be affected by the philosophy of guidance professed. For instance, is guidance concerned primarily with the full-blown problem of the individual, or is it equally important to work towards prevention? We hear a great deal about developmental guidance these days. If we accept this type of approach to guidance, the program we adopt will be considerably different from programs which were established before the emergence of these new ideas.

Size of the School System

The final condition which I wish to draw to your attention as influencing the guidance progam is the size of the school system and the consequent problem of the kind of organization that fits the size. A large school system will require a considerable amount of organization. In New York City it is necessary to have thirty district guidance coordinators, one for each of the local school districts. While formerly there was a supervisory staff for guidance in each of the five boroughs of New York City, today because of the rapid extension of the program there are two supervisors in each borough, in addition to a director and an assistant director for the whole guidance program. Of course, where the community is not as large as this one, the guidance organization may run the whole gamut from the director of guidance for a three level system with many counselors at each level to a director of guidance who in fact is the single counselor in a senior high school.

GUIDANCE IN A LARGE URBAN CENTER

Having seen the background conditions for guidance, let us try to assemble a picture of the guidance program in a large urban community. Let us start with the elementary school.

Elementary School

In New York City we believe that a professionally staffed program should be a part of every elementary school organization. With due respect to Frank Parsons and those who first developed the guidance program on the secondary school level, we recognize that to achieve results with children preventive work must begin before problems are manifest. This happens generally in the third or fourth grade. As a matter of fact, we try to begin our work two or three weeks before the child is enrolled in kindergarten. We hope that the guidance counselor assigned to an elementary school will succeed in meeting with the parents of the children who are entering kindergarten, and in our culturally deprived areas, the pre-kindergarten class.

What is our major work in the elementary school guidance program? In general, the activity consists of the identification of students who are considerably different from their peers, the appraisal of student abilities and problems, teacher education so that they can understand children better, work with parents, and the development of referral sources to help children who need services which the schools cannot offer.

In the elementary school guidance program the emphasis at present is on prevention. Of course, this stress parallels the current focus in the mental health movement. The idea is that it is more efficient to attempt to prevent problems, rather than dealing with them. For example, when a young person at the age of fifteen is three, four or five grades behind in his reading level, there is relatively little that can be done for him in this regard, and whatever can be done will be rather costly. Of course, such a young person has usually suffered emotionally and otherwise because of this long standing deprivation. But if this retardation could be detected in the third or fourth grade and if work could be started with him at this level, the youngster would undoubtedly be brought up to grade level and thus the emotional and other problems flowing from this deprivation would be avoided.

To achieve the goals which were just mentioned an adequate staff with appropriate training is essential. At present we do not expect the counselor-pupil ratio in the elementary schools to be the same as that which is being recommended for the secondary schools. Though recommendations are being made that there should be one fully trained counselor for each 250 pupils in the secondary school, it seems adequate that there be one guidance counselor for every elementary school with a 600 to 1000 student population. Of course, special situations in certain schools may have different requirements.

Now that the work and goals of elementary school guidance have been reviewed, it is appropriate to present an overall picture of the different programs being carried out at this level. At this point three programs will be discussed: the Early Identification and Prevention Program, the Playgroup Program, and Junior Guidance; the Higher Horizons Program which also operates in the elementary schools will be described later.

The Early Identification and Prevention Program was decided on as a demonstration of the special purposes of guidance in the elementary school. Thirty-seven schools were chosen in which a counselor was assigned full time, and a psychologist and social worker were assigned half time. These three professionals used the team approach in their work with children and their parents. The team goes into the second grade classes so that they might recognize problems that a teacher may ignore because there may be no obvious disciplinary problem involved. Thus the withdrawn children are identified early. Futhermore, as a standard operating procedure, the team reviews the teachers' appraisals or anecdotal records. They also interview children who indicate some potential difficulty as well as those who show signs of talents which should be developed. The identification of this latter group, the gifted, enables the school system to work early with the very bright youngsters who perhaps are not being challenged in the regular classroom.

While the Early Identification and Prevention Program has won some acclaim, there is a major problem associated with it: the lack of sufficient staff to introduce this approach in the other five hundred and thirty-five elementary schools. Another draw-back of the program is that adequate referral sources are not available. As the team uncovers problems they wish to direct students to sources of assistance in reading, speech, mental health and other areas. The referral agencies are not available in suf-ficient numbers to help the children whose problems have been identified. While some members of the school staff become dis-couraged by this situation, others with a great deal of initiative and resourcefulness have been able to locate help for these young people. I wish to state, categorically, that the lack of sufficient services is not a good basis for doing away with the Early Iden-tification and Prevention Program. When more people hear their cries, more and more doors which are now closed to them will be opened.

A second special program that I should like to discuss is the Play Group Program. It is carried out by counselors under the supervision of a highly qualified group therapist. In some twelve schools there are twenty-five groups, with five or six children in each, who meet with the counselor once a week in a special room set aside for this purpose. The children engage in what might be called unstructured play, with the trained counselor making the appropriate observations and imposing limits when necessary. Note that the counselor is not referred to as a therapist. The counselor does group work with six children once a week. The children involved in the program are those who present problems to the school as a whole and to their respective teach-ers in particular. One aspect of the program that appeals to me is that from time to time luncheon sessions are held with the teach-ers of these children. The supervising therapist leads the meeting. As an observer at such sessions I noted that the teachers gain a deeper understanding of the problems which moved the children to act out in the classroom, and, of course, they reached a deeper understanding of the psychodynamics of children. No expansion of this program is foreseen, however, since not enough counselors have the training to lead such a group effectively. This type of activity is not within the purview of the school-oriented guidance counselor who generally has not had clinical training. An excel-lent description of this entire program has been provided by Schiffer, [1] the supervising therapist.

Another elementary school program called Junior Guidance is concerned primarily with instruction rather than guidance. However, guidance is very much involved in it. The goal of the program is therapeutic education for children who are either emotionally disturbed or socially maladjusted. The term "emotionally disturbed" is not used here in a medical sense, because not all of the children have been diagnosed as such; but from a clinical point of view they give indication of being emotionally disturbed. Certainly they are socially maladjusted in the sense that they would not be containable in a school setting if they were not placed through this program in classes of from 8 to 10 children. In some parts of the program there are three teachers serving 25 to 28 children; two of the teachers actually instruct at any one time and the third acts as the relief teacher with responsibility for anecdotal records and similar work. This program also involves group counseling for parents.

It should be of some interest to observers to learn the distribution of the counselors' time in the Junior Guidance program. Individual counseling of students receives 15% of their working day; counseling parents consumes 35% of their time, working with teachers 30%, group counseling 5%, and referral contacts 15%.

The Junior Guidance program is steadily being expanded in New York City, and today there are approximately 62 schools with 217 teachers and 1800 pupils enrolled in these special classes. The program is attracting a great deal of attention because school systems throughout the country are very much concerned about organizing classes for their disturbed children and universities are co-operating by preparing teachers for classes of such children. Furthermore, state legislatures have been passing laws making it obligatory on the part of school districts to maintain classes for these children, rather than to have them exempt from instruction.

Problems in Elementary School Guidance

In the above brief survey of guidance in the elementary school in a large urban center we looked at the Early Identification and Prevention Program, the Play Group Program and the Group Guidance Program. In the background of all of these programs there are certain problems which guidance personnel should consider. The solution of these problems in local situations will go a long way to clarifying the role and function of the staff involved, and consequently the training and screening of applicants will be facilitated. The first of these problems is this: is it better to have a guidance counselor in the elementary schools along the lines of the New York City schools, or might it be desirable to employ a school psychologist, following the model of many of the suburban districts? If you have both, what are the areas in which the two will overlap even when their respective duties have been carefully demarcated? Perhaps those school systems which have not as yet plunged into a decision in this area would profit by conferring with the staff and line workers in systems which are operating according to these different methods.

A second important problem relative to guidance in the elementary school is a trend on the part of some counselors toward activities which they are not really prepared to perform. Specifically, I refer to an attempt to do "amateur psychotherapy" with children. It is not too difficult to understand the reasons for these attempts. When there is a shortage of therapists both in the school system and in community agencies, and the counselor is faced with young people who cry to him for help, it is hard for him to resist "trying his best." He reasons that "some help is better than no help at all." It is pertinent to note that Dr. Gordon of Yeshiva University, who has done much work on the culturally disadvantaged child, is reported in the press to have addressed himself to this problem. He calls on counselors to put greater emphasis on their relationship to teachers, to parents, and to groups of children, rather than concerning themselves with psychotherapy. Of course, whenever there is need for psychotherapy it should be provided in the appropriate setting and by those who have received professional preparation.

A third problem which I wish to mention here may occur at any school level but is faced most often in the elementary school level. It is that of the counselor functioning as a teacher-educator without engaging in supervision. Dr. Loughran wisely referred to the interrelationships of school staff members in developing, organizing and administering guidance programs. It is true that we talk about the counselor as a person who is attempting to develop in teachers an understanding of children. In doing this he is a teacher-educator. But this activity produces a series of related problems, some of which are the following. Do teachers resent the counselor's working with them towards increased understanding of children? Just what part does a counselor play in working with a teacher who has mishandled a child? How does he do this without arrogating to himself the aura of the supervisor? Certainly counselors would agree that they are not supervisors of teachers. The counselor's activity as a teacher educator uncovers a sensitive area involving personnel relationships. It certainly deserves further research and study.

Junior High School

Now let us turn our attention to guidance in the junior high school. Here the counselor's work follows the traditional aspects of guidance in which the emphasis is on vocational exploration, along with the identification of students with problems, appraisal of the abilities and personality of students, work with teachers and parents, and the appropriate referral of students to outside specialists.

At the completion of his junior high school course the student must make a choice of high schools, and he may have a large number from which to choose. The work of the counselor in the junior high school is to help the young person to make the decision which best reflects his vocational goal. For example, in New York City the child who is not going to college and wants to go into industry may choose among 29 vocational high schools, some of which are highly specialized. If a child selects the School of Printing he is pretty much deciding at the age of 15 that he would like to spend the rest of his vocational life in the printing industry. Many small communities fortunately, and I say fortunately advisedly, do not have schools which are so specialized. Yet the choice of the high school program is very often conditioned, even at the age of 15 by the vocational goals of the student, and the counselor in these smaller districts must assist the young person in making this choice.

There are two special problems with which the counselor in the junior high school is concerned: articulation and discipline. Articulation is distinctive at this level because the counselor works with the staffs and the students of both the feeding elementary school and with the high school to which the graduates are going. The counselor spends a considerable amount of his time at articulation. Discipline is also an important factor at this level. Disciplinary problems of children are usually most serious at this level, and for this reason one hears much talk about the junior high school as the most difficult place in which to teach. And children of this age group should be expected to have social and emotional problems. The counselor is often involved in these, even though he should not be thought of as involved in a disciplinary role. Certainly, if a child is considered a continual discipline problem the counselor must become involved even if a dean or an assistant principal is the one who handles such a child initially. [2]

In a large urban setting there will at times be a need for the institution of "difficult" schools. Students are assigned to these schools on the basis of attendance or disciplinary problems. To cope with the needs of these students it is necessary to increase the professional staff such that clinical help can be provided. The team approach which is often implied in the term "pupil personnel services" is utilized. In this case the counselor is really a team member of the larger group. There is room for considerable research regarding developments in these difficult schools.

The "Career Guidance" program may be examined to illustrate the special programs which have been established to resolve specific problems in the junior high schools. This program is intended for young people who have already indicated that they will not succeed in completing a high school education. Many of them are just waiting for their sixteenth birthday so that they can leave school. These are the pupils who have failed a number of subjects and are retarded three and four years in reading and arithmetic. The Career Guidance program directs itself towards these young people either for their continuing in school, or if leaving school is inevitable, for preparing them for their first job. Classes for these children are distinctive in that they are small, with 12 to 15 pupils in each class, and they are taught by special guidance-oriented teachers. The students may take two or three classes with other children but spend most of their day with their special home teacher. After school jobs are found for these pupils in an attempt to give them the self-respect which they seem to need. Classes in occupational information and job attitudes are integral parts of the Career Guidance Program. Special curriculum materials which aim at heightening students' motivation, have been developed for these classes. This is a steadily growing program. In 1957-58 only one hundred and nine pupils were enrolled in it, but in 1962-63 the number had soared to one thousand, seven hundred and eighty-two.

Senior High School

Having seen the guidance picture in the elementary school and junior high school, let us now turn to the senior high schools, academic and vocational. I would like to share with you a consideration of some of the problems in regard to guidance which face the New York City school system at this level. Of course, other areas have similar problems of the type which I mention. First, there is an organizational problem in regard to the teacher-counselor. I refer to the tradition of part-time counseling carried on by teachers. Many of these teachers are well prepared for their guidance work, but the concept has been that "You are a teacher first; you spend two or three periods a day teaching your subject and then you spend the rest of the day counseling." The New York City focus in participating in the New York State Project ABLE [3] was an attempt to demonstrate through working with children from culturally disadvantaged areas that full-time counseling had decided advantages over part-time counseling. Project ABLE will continue for five years but New York City was successful in securing full-time counseling in the high schools before the completion of the Project. Nevertheless, a considerable amount of work still remains to be done in the area of successfully organizing the guidance program in the high schools on the basis of both full-time and part-time counselors.

A second problem which is connected with the senior high school guidance program is the use of the guidance generalist or the guidance specialist. For instance, should college guidance be handled by every counselor who works with groups coming up from the ninth or tenth year, or should college orientation be handled only by a specialist in this field for the eleventh and twelfth year students? A similar situation exists with regard to the counseling of prospective dropouts. Should these young people be turned over to somebody who specializes in this work? Again, 'there are work experience programs, e.g. STEP [4] which have guidance aspects. Should this activity be turned over to the specialist or to the generalist? There are many things to be said pro and con with regard to this problem, and more research seems to be required. If the final decision is in favor of the specialist it is obvious that there will be important implications for the counselor education institutions. And if the specialist is preferred, it is hoped that the organization within the school will veer toward the pupil personnel team approach which I mentioned with regard to the junior high schools.

An additional problem of guidance in the senior high school centers on a recent shift of emphasis in this work. Certainly it was with good purpose that personal and social guidance have been added to the educational and vocational work of the counselor. However I find, as I get around to more high schools, that counselors have gone overboard in these new areas and that too few high schools are giving enough emphasis to vocational guidance. As a result, the college-bound student is provided for, the prospective dropout very often is getting even a greater share of time, but the young person who is preparing to work immediately after high school, is ignored in many schools. Counselors in too many instances are not paying enough attention to the kind of work this young person is going to do and how he should prepare for his job. Among other things, better use could be made of certain subjects which are taken by many of these pupils, particularly Home Economics and Industrial Arts. Guidance for occupations could be integrated into these and some other courses. However, there is a notable tendency to transfer the vocational guidance aspect of the counselor's work to the New York State Employment Service.

Perhaps the reason for the guidance counselors' minimizing their function in vocational guidance is a natural result of the extensive services preformed by the New York State Employment Service. This service provides fifty counselors for forty academic high schools and eleven vocational high schools. Students who avail themselves of this service may obtain pre-testing interviews, testing with the General Aptitude Test Battery, a proficiency test in stenography and typewriting, as well as employ-

ment counseling and placement.[5] Seniors, part-time students
and prospective dropouts are served through this agency. The
NYSES came into the schools mainly as a placement agency and
works with the young person when he has already decided to go
to work. I should like to add that many of their personnel workers do a good counseling job. This additional service has been
very beneficial to the local guidance program. Of course, this
state employment service operates in each of the states, as it is
financed by the federal government. Though it is a great boon
when it operates in the schools, it is my conviction that the
regular guidance personnel must be on their guard lest they fail
in one of their fundamental tasks, vocational guidance, just because one aspect of it is well handled by the state agency.

Special Education and Guidance

Now that we have surveyed the general guidance practices
and problems at the three levels in the public school system of
New York City, I would like to give an overview of some of the
areas of special education and their relationship to the guidance
and counseling staffs. I am going to mention work with the
socially and emotionally maladjusted, the physically handicapped, the mentally retarded, pupils transferred from custodial
institutions, pupils who are being tried by the courts, and unmarried mothers.

Mention was made above of Junior Guidance, the program
for the socially maladjusted in the elementary schools. Corres-
ponding to this program for pupils from grades five to ten are
the "600" schools. Such schools have been functioning for the
boys and girls who present grave emotional and behavior problems, and for whom current procedures in the regular schools
have been unsuccessful. Counselors in these schools spend a
large share of their time in screening applications for admission.
New York City also maintains "600" schools in treatment centers throughout the state but does not provide guidance service
in such residential institutions. The school system provides the
teaching services but is firmly convinced that guidance service
in an institutional setting should be made available by the institution itself because such service must be in accord with the
philosophy of the institution and consistent with that provided

in the living quarters. Of course, this is a moot question and one that the workshops could pofitably discuss. Many of these institutions have made demands on the city for guidance personnel and clinical service but we have resisted them in this matter. However, in our "600" program the city does provide guidance services with a ratio of one counselor to approximately 125 to 150 pupils.

Physically handicapped children need special guidance service. Our counselors who have a working relationship with the Division of Vocational Rehabilitation help teachers with sources of referral, both public and private. They also work with parents to have them understand the limitations of their children and how they can adjust to these limitations. Due to various limiting factors guidance personnel can do little intensive counseling of these students except on a few special cases. For the visually handicapped there is a special counselor trained in this area who counsels students in sight conservation and Braille classes, and arranges for special examinations in Braille for these young people as they advance in their education, in addition to performing the other appropriate work of guidance for these children.

Several programs exist in New York City for the mentally retarded. For one thing special classes are organized for them. They are called CRMD (children with retarded mental development) and TMR (trainable mentally retarded) classes. The teachers of these classes play the major role in the guidance of these students and they assist these children through concern for both the problem of normal children and adjustment to the special problems involved with their limited mental capacity. In 1963-64 there were 11,447 pupils in CRMD classes. There are seven full-time counselors who work with these children. These seven are specialists for the counselors in the schools. They are essentially resource persons for the regular counselors, often helping them to obtain assistance from appropriate agencies. There is also a successful program of job placement for retarded children and work experience programs for them have been initiated.

In the first section of this paper reference was made to the special needs of children returning from custodial institutions among the factors that influence a guidance program. In New York City this is a question of placing 1200 such young people, who come from the state hospitals. Those who are of elementary or junior high school age are assigned to an appropriate school setting by the district guidance coordinators. For the secondary schools there is a city-wide office wherein guidance counselors interview the youngsters. Working with the social workers from the institutions involved, this office tries to place the children in schools which will best serve their needs. In 1964-65 there were 1218 children who were thus cared for in the high schools.

To complete the picture of the problems and the type of approach used to assist the young people who are faced with these problems, I wish to mention briefly work with children who are before the courts, unmarried mothers and those who speak Spanish but not English. Among children in the courts, delinquincy cases are most notable; for instance, on May 31, 1965 there was a case load of about 9,000 active delinquincy cases. Eighteen guidance workers are assigned to work with these children; their task requires them to notify the schools of the court action, and to interpret the court's decision to the school. Unmarried mothers are interviewed after delivery to decide the best placement so that they might continue their education. The school experience has been that it is essential in certain areas to include among the staff who have been called substitute auxiliary teachers. All of these personnel are Spanish-speaking and have had experience in community work with Puerto Rican families. They are usually Puerto Ricans themselves who have completed professional courses in guidance. Guidance is one basic area of their work.

TWO GUIDANCE PROJECTS

The guidance function in the three levels of the schools and in the special education areas of a large urban center have been briefly sketched. It would seem appropriate to finish this report with a description of two projects which are intimately related with guidance: the Demonstration Guidance Project and the Higher Horizons program. First, it is necessary to explain the distinction between the two programs. A great deal of publicity has been given to Higher Horizons, but unfortunately too often the outcomes of the Demonstration Guidance Project have been attributed to Higher Horizons. The Demonstration Guidance Project was the pilot program which inspired Higher Horizons.

The Demonstration Guidance Project

The Demonstration Guidance Project was instituted in one junior high school, Junior High School #43, and in one senior high school, George Washington High School and began in 1956. The Higher Horizons on the other hand was begun in the elementary grades in 1959 and includes fifty-two elementary schools, thirteen junior high schools and eleven high schools. In the Demonstration Guidance Project only one half (the more able group) of the school population in the junior high school was included in the program, while all children in the schools which have the program are included in Higher Horizons. The goal of the Demonstration Guidance Project was the students' graduation from high school with an academic diploma and their admission into college, while Higher Horizons seeks the wider goal of better education and wider fields of choice for disadvantaged children. These differences have been summarized in the Table 3.

TABLE 3

**Differences Between Higher Horizons
and the Demonstration Guidance Project ***

	DEMONSTRATION GUIDANCE PROJECT	HIGHER HORIZONS PROGRAM
Begun	September 1956	September 1959
Initial Grades	7, 8, 9 (jr. h. s.)	3 (elem.), 7 (jr. h. s.)
Extension	to senior high school in September 1957	one elementary and one secondary grade added each year
Schools	Jr. H. S. 43; George Washington H. S.	52 elementary schools 13 jr. high schools 11 high schools
Target Population	the academically able	all children
Goal	graduation with academic diploma; college admission	better education and wider fields of choice for disadvantaged children
Present Status	completed in June 1962	64,075 pupils in grades 3 to 10

* based on Table 1 in J. Landers' *Higher Horizons, Progress Report,* p. 5.

In the Demonstration Guidance Project the purpose was to reverse the trend whereby young people in disadvantaged areas become more and more retarded in their school work and show increasingly poor results when compared to national norms for children their age. This change was meant to be effected by providing concentrated instruction and increased guidance services for these young people. In implementing these plans, an additional teacher was assigned to the junior high schools for every one hundred and sixty children, and an additional teacher was assigned to the high schools for every thirty children. As a result, the high school was able to have classes with as few as fifteen students in mathematics and English. Thus the teachers and students could concentrate on those skill subjects in which the disadvantaged child is generally retarded. The guidance program was recognized as the keystone of the project and the central activity of the counselors was seen to be the counseling interview. Due to increased staff, there was a guidance ratio of one to one hundred and twenty-five (vs. one to one thousand, five hundred in the junior high school) and in addition the clinical services of psychologists were provided in the school building. Some students had as many as twenty extended interviews. Another element of the program involved field trips to colleges, the ballet, the theatre, concerts and museums. In addition, special work with parents was done. And the head of the guidance program put much effort into college placement.

What were the results of the Demonstration Guidance Project? To answer this question it would be profitable to compare the 1957-1959 classes in the George Washington High School coming from the same Junior High School No. 43 with the classes of 1960-1962. Whereas for the earlier classes only forty-three pupils completed the academic diploma requirements, for the project classes one hundred and eight did so. Whereas in the pre-project classes there were some forty-four failures, the number of failures in the project classes was fourteen. A scholastic average of eighty percent or higher was achieved by only thirteen pupils in the pre-project groups, but thirty-seven pupils in the project classes achieved a scholastic average of eighty percent or higher. While in the pre-project group no pupil in a three year period came above the rank of fifty-one in class standing of some eight hundred graduates, in the project classes there were seven pupils who ranked among the top ten in the three graduating classes, three in the 1960 class, two in the 1961 class and two in the 1962 class. Furthermore, eighty-nine percent of the pupils who earned academic diplomas continued their education in institutions of higher learning. Another noteworthy fact is that only twenty-two percent of those originally in the project became dropouts, and this percentage is well below the school dropout rate and one-third lower than that noted in the city as a whole. [6]

What are the implications of the Demonstration Guidance Project? In general, it was demonstrated that students in disadvantaged areas *can* be prepared for college or other advanced education. However, it seems that they need the whole formula which was prescribed for these students, and the formula was based on compensating for his background. The small classes without the intensive guidance would not suffice. This is equally true of the cultural expeditions and the involvement of parents. The central role of the guidance program for these students must be recognized. The counselors should be fully trained and have a case load not to exceed one hundred and twenty-five pupils each. The counseling should be intensive because students in disadvantaged areas are likely to face more serious personal problems than other children do, and instruction will be impaired if the children are not aided with these problems. Motivation, as it is with all people, is essential and must be constantly worked for since these young people start off with a feeling that they cannot succeed. Within the bounds of realistic aspirations, the pupils in disadvantaged areas can be brought to realize that success in school in all levels is possible.

Higher Horizons

Higher Horizons is really an outgrowth of the Demonstration Guidance Project. It is now taking place in fifty-two elementary schools, thirteen junior high schools and eleven senior high schools. Unfortunately, however, it was not possible to make available the same program and personnel that was given to the Demonstration Guidance Project. In dollars and cents, in the pilot program approximately $250 to $270 additional to the usual cost of educating the child was spent. In the Higher Horizons program, where almost sixty-five thousand are involved, from $60 to $75 additional to the usual cost of educating the child is being spent. Of course, it is entirely too early to assess the success of the Higher Horizons program, since the children involved are now only entering the tenth year in high school.

SOME UNRESOLVED QUESTIONS

In closing, I would like to pose some questions, based in part on the material mentioned above, for your consideration. What is the function of the guidance counselor in relation to other pupil personnel services? Should there be a clear line of demarcation between the functions of the guidance counselor and those of the school social worker, the school psychologist and attendance teacher? If we must avoid overlapping among these functionaries, how can this be done without imposing inflexible and unrealistic walls between the work of these staff members? How can their work be coordinated? Must limits be imposed on the services of each of them, and if so how can such limitation be achieved?

There are questions of policy. What part should guidance play in the integration movement? How is guidance concerned with the demand for programs to compensate for the disadvantages faced by minority youth? In the effort to help the minority youth, are there too few counselors and teachers working with children in middle class sections so that such students are neglected? What responsibility does a school system and its guidance personnel have for the breaking down of racial and religious barriers that exist in employment? Specifically, does a counselor take the initiative in breaking down such barriers when they exist in an apprenticeship program? How much leadership does the guidance staff take for making sure that young people reach their real potential for educational growth?

REFERENCES

1. Schiffer, M. The Use of the Seminar in Training Teachers and Counselors as leaders of Therapeutic Play Groups for Maladjusted Children. *American Journal of Ortho-psychiatry.* January, 1960, 154-165.

2. Concerning discipline and guidance cf.: Williamson, E. G. and Foley, J. D. *Counseling and Discipline*. New York: McGraw-Hill, 1949, and Bernhardt, K. S. *Discipline and Child Guidance*. New York: McGraw-Hill, 1964.

3. *Project ABLE, the First Year*. Albany, N. Y.: The State Education Department, Univ. of the State of New York, 1963. Also, *Project ABLE, an Appraisal*. Same source, 1964.

4. *STEP, The School to Employment Program, Cases in Point*. New York State Education Dept.: Albany, N. Y., 1964.

5. *Sixty-Fourth Annual Report of the Superintendent of Schools, 1961-1962*. New York: Board of Education, 1963.

6. Hillson, H. T. and Myers, Florence C. *The Demonstration Guidance Project, 1957-1962*. New York: George Washington H. S., 1963.

7. Landers, J. *Higher Horizons, Progress Report*. New York: Board of Education, 1963.

ADDITIONAL REFERENCES

Guidance for Special Groups of Pupils:

New York City Youth Board, *Youth in New York City - Out of School and Out of Work*, 79 Madison Avenue, New York, 1962.

New York State Division for Youth, *The School Drop Out Problem in Major Cities of New York State*, Part 1, Rochester, 2-Syracuse, 270 Broadway, New York, 1962-1963.

School Guidance for Urban Areas in Transition:

Chandler, B.J., Stiles, L.J. and Kitsuse, J.I., *Education in Urban Society*, Dodd, Mead, New York, 1962.

Conant, J.B., *Slums and Suburbs*, McGraw Hill, New York, 1961.

Educational Policies Commission, *Education and the Disadvantaged*, National Educational Association, Washington D.C., 1962.

Foster, C.R., *Guidance for Today's Schools*, Gin and Co., Boston, 1957.

Passow, A. Harry, *Education in Depressed Areas*, Teachers College, Columbia University, New York, 1963.

Riessman, F., *The Culturally Deprived Child*, Harper and Brothers, New York, 1962.

State Department of Education, *Reducing the School Drop Out Rate—A Report on the Holding Power Project*, Bureau of Guidance, State Education Department,. Albany, New York.

Tanneyhill, A., *From School to Job: Guidance for Minority Youth*, Public Affairs Committee, New York, 1953.

THE INCREASING COMPLEXITY AND
VALUE OF VOCATIONAL COUNSELING

SALVATORE G. DIMICHAEL
*Regional Representative, United States Vocational
Rehabilitation Administration*

*There has been a tendency of late on the part of some writers
to sing dirges for the on-coming death of vocational guidance. Dr.
DiMichael challenges this attitude. Instead, he maintains that during
the past half century of its existence vocational guidance has established a history of progressive growth. In the days of Frank Parsons
the vocational counselor was required to study but for one, two, or
three terms; today there is a drive towards the certifying of counselors
at least at the master's degree. An additional area of change has been
the counselor's concern for the integration of personality factors and
problems in the occupational development of his clients.*

Although the modern guidance movement had no single
formative source, [1] some people regarded 1959 as the year of its
fiftieth anniversary. This date was justified in light of the influence of the posthumous publication, in 1909, of the book by
Frank Parsons on, *Choosing a Vocation.* Another likely anniversary date is 1963, fifty years after the formation of the
National Vocational Guidance Association. These and other
birthdays have been the occasion for reviews of past major
events, attempts to view the current status of progress in the
perspective of history and predictions of avenues of most
fruitful possible progress. Some of us engaged in this field
may voice the opinion that the amount of progress is as-
tonishing, or at least substantial; others may believe that our
advancement has been small in view of our everyday observa-
tion that our counseling assistance is modest indeed in improving the lives of our actual and potential clients.

I would like to offer my view of some important contributions during the past fifty years, with attention to major trends in present practice. The picture from which I abstract my observations is complex and far-flung, yet I will have to attempt to simplify its meaning, if we are to attempt to see our present practices in perspective within the space limit of this paper.

A HISTORICAL PERSPECTIVE

Writing in 1909, Frank Parsons proposed that guidance be conceived as a three-fold concept: helping the person to understand himself, to have a realistic knowledge of occupations, and to arrive at a choice in which there would be a matching of the two sets of factors. Parsons proposed that the qualifications for such work should be set in terms of a high school education, two years of practical experience, maturity of personality such that a person should be at least twenty-five years of age, and a special course of one, two or three terms, according to the ability and previous preparation of the student.

The guidance movement was begun by workers who were social and civic-minded, but soon in the decade of the 1910's was accepted by some of the larger public schools, by the graduate schools and research centers in the 1920's, and by large public and private agencies thereafter. The field has retained a characteristic concern for dealing with practical problems of its clients, in their present as well as future adjustment. [2] In fact, it has been frequently said that follow-up studies are the best criteria of the effectiveness of guidance methods.

Counselor Education

The training of guidance workers obviously has become far more demanding. As long ago as 1937, Patterson of Minnesota stated that: "The modern guidance worker must be thoroughly grounded in psychology, in research and statistics, and in clinical procedures. An M.S. degree in psychometrics or its equivalent would appear to be a minimum essential. The Ph.D. degree or its equivalent would appear to be a desirable qualification." [3] In the current situation, the training of vocational counselors is far broader than advocated by Patterson. The Master's Degree is regarded as a prerequisite for professional status in the National Vocational Guidance Association, with appropriate experience of at least three years. The Ph.D. is required for counseling positions in the Veterans Administration and is frequently possessed by personnel workers in colleges and universities. The vocational counselor is being regarded more and more as a specialist with technicians to assist him. However, there are some authorities who emphasize the need to prepare teachers for general guidance and some counseling functions. Others advocate emphasis on the Master's Degree as the most suitable training prerequisite for the large majority of counselors, because there is such a desperate need for their services in so many public and private agencies. Briefly stated, there is no general consensus as yet on the content of counselor's training, on the appropriate breadth of his knowledge and skills, nor on the minimum level of graduate work. However, the inclusion of an internship as a part of graduate training is more prevalent than ever. About two thirds of the graduate institutions required internship experience before 1962; the number will increase. [2]

The Testing Movement

In the 1920's the guidance movement incorporated the use of group intelligence and achievement tests within its framework. The success of classification tests in the armed forces during the first World War, and the need for scientific tools to help in the analysis of the individual, brought about their ready acceptance in guidance work. The advent of such tests was heralded widely, and so over-enthusiastically that some people dared to believe that the process of matching people and jobs could become almost mechanical. A somewhat severe reaction against psychometrics took pace in the late 1920's but later developments in psychological tests, and their successful use during the depression and second World War, have made for a more realistic appraisal of their value.

During the depression years a large number of vocational aptitude and achievement tests were developed, such as at the Minnesota Employment Stabilization Research Institute, and the Rochester Employment Project. These made a distinct contribution to guidance by showing that persons selected on the basis of abilities, interest and aptitudes performed better on the job, and were better satisfied with their occupational adjustment.

In graduate training schools of the 1930's and early 1940's, considerable emphasis was placed on the limitation of tests and their technical character, with the result that counselors and counselor-trainees were not encouraged to interpret test scores in counseling interviews. Moreover, leaders in guidance advocated that the tests to be administered should be selected by the guidance worker. The strong trend since then has been in the direction of providing results of test scores to subjects, to have them understand the meaning of group tests administered, and explain the meaning of the scores in group or class meetings. School leaders increasingly advocate that test scores should be given to students with suitable explanations.

In terms of an individualized approach to counseling, a number of articles have appeared recently advocating a maximum of client participation in discussing and full choice in selecting tests which the client would take under the administration of the psychologist or psychometrist. The proposal, in its most extreme form, was made by Bordin and Bixler, and Bixler and Bixler. [4] The claim is made that the client accepts the test results more readily and less defensively. This proposal does not seem to have been widely accepted; however, counselors are convinced that test scores should be provided to clients. The question today is how to do it in the most effective way.

Several studies on the use of psychological tests serve to highlight the fact that tests results should be made known to the individual in counseling if they are to have effect on job satisfaction. Two significant studies show no effect on job satisfaction tion. Two significant studies showed no effect on job satisfaction if test scores are not used in counseling. Thus, E. L. Thorndike reported no correlation between the test data obtained by students 13 to 15 years of age and vocational success after a ten year follow-up. And Latham reported on a one-year follow-up of high-school seniors given 27 aptitude tests. He found no greater satisfaction or success as reported by employer ratings by those whose work was more appropriate, or less appropriate, to their aptitudes

By contrast, other investigations disclosed a positive effect upon job adjustment when test scores were used in and with counseling. Thus, some three decades ago, British psychologists [7] conducted a two-year follow-up of 1639 secondary school students and a four-year follow-up of 603 students. All received counseling, but half of them were based on test information. The students who were tested and informed of the results made a better work adjustment than the non-tested. Job shifts among the tested-counseled group were in the direction of "accordance" with tests scores while the other group tended to shift away from recommended jobs. It seems that clients need to be convinced of the evidence on which counseling recommendations are made, if the counseling is to be effective.

The improvements in psychological tests as counseling tools have played a significant role in the past half century of guidance work. In present counseling practice, group and individual tests of intelligence, achievement and vocational aptitudes have become very widely used. Interest inventories have become more popular in recent years, due in large measure to the persistent and fruitful research of such people as Strong, Kuder and Darley. The interest inventories have been especially useful in predicting future occupational fields, greater job permanence in the areas of primary interest, and directions of job shifts.

On the other hand, personality inventories have not fulfilled their promise of the early years. Counselors know too well the many difficulties in interpreting the results to the client. When used, the personality inventories may help the counselor to know the client better, and the results serve as background information on which to plan counseling approaches. Projective tools have become controversial and are used with even greater caution than personality inventories by most counselors. Since projective tools attempt to assess subconscious or unconscious factors in the client's personality, their results serve as helps to the counselor in determining suitable counseling approaches.

OCCUPATIONAL INFORMATION IN COUNSELING

In the early days of the guidance movement, the counselor had to learn about occupations by field visits and observations. Today, the counselor could spend all his time between interviews just in reading the reams of occupational information in printed form, if he would or could survive it. To help his client understand the world of work, and the requirements of likely jobs, it is imperative to have accurate information. The difficulty in attaining proficiency in this area is that there are over thirty-five thousand documented types of job titles. Not even a job analyst could make a first-hand study of them all in a lifetime.

By virtue of an enormous effort by guidance workers and job analyst specialists, occupational information is available today in well classified form, in quality, and is being constantly rewritten, refined and kept recent. The effort requires the resources of the Federal and State governments, as well as qualified specialists in various fields, who do their research and writing in contractual arrangements with publishing houses. Particulary worthy of mention are the *Dictionary of Occupational Titles,* and the revised issues of the *Occupational Handbook,* both prepared by the U.S. Department of Labor. Job information is analyzed and kept up to date by State and Federal agencies, as well as private publishing houses, and more recently by various industries and labor unions.

The impetus for such a systematized array of occupational materials dates back to the later days of the depression of the 1930's. With the increase in occupational materials, there have been continuous efforts to use it more effectively. Career days have become fairly well established in schools, and are based almost entirely on furnishing occupational data of potential interest to certain groups of students. Career days have also sought to sensitize students on the need and value of individual counseling. Such broadscaled attempts have assumed that the dissemination of reliable job data would make people choose more suitable careers. Yet, the research evidence strongly indicates that counseling is necessary if job information is to be used to the person's advantage.

Stone [8] described the results of an experiment with college students, in which a control group had no vocational orientation course, another group had the course, and a sub-group of the latter had counseling in addition. The results showed that the orientation group had more knowledge of occupations, and made a slightly better record in realistic job choices. The sub-group who had the orientation course and counseling, made a decidedly better record. We see once again the superiority of counseling in combination with guidance tools in improving job adjustment. During the last decade, far more attention is being devoted to the psychological aspects of using occupational information in the counseling interview. This current trend seems to have been given renewed impetus by an article by Brayfield. [9] He raised serious questions about the efficacy of courses in occupational information, without an individualized counseling experience. He explored the systematic treatment of occupational information in terms of informational, readjustive, motivational applications. Moreover, he emphasized the principle that "any use of occupational information should be preceded by individual diagnosis." Thus, Brayfield would say, first, the counselor should know his client, then he should provide occupational information as the psychological needs of the client indicates, then the counseling may rightly lead to appropriate job choice and plans for pursuing a suitable career as a part of a total plan of life.

GUIDANCE, COUNSELING AND PSYCHOTHERAPY IN VOCATIONAL COUNSELING

In 1924, the National Vocational Guidance Association defined vocational guidance as the "giving of information, experience and advice in regard to choosing an occupation, preparing for it, entering it, and progressing in it." The definition reflects a lack of scientific tools, the relative unawareness of the extent of individual difference, and lots of emphasis on the activity and experience of the guidance worker. The definition did not seem to satisfy the Association and was revised in 1930 and again in 1937 to emphasize activity by the client.

> Vocational guidance is the process of assisting the individual to choose an occupation, prepare for it, enter upon and progress in it. It is concerned primarily with helping individuals make decisions and choices ivolved in planning a future and building a career—decisions and choices necessary in effecting satisfactory vocational adjustment.

The emphasis on helping clients to make decisions and choices was so deliberately intended that the words are re-

peated several times in the two-sentence definition. The availability of improved psychometric tools served to enhance the
role of the guidance worker as a competent collector of personal
information about the individual, and as a psychological diag-
nostician.

The Clinical vs. Non-Directive Controversy

In 1939, Williamson proposed a systematic basis for
clinical, as distingushed from traditional, counseling in terms
of a six-step process. The steps were: analysis, or collecting data;
synthesis, or summarizing data; diagnosis, or describing major
strengths and weaknesses of the client in comparison with occupational requirements; prognosis, or alternative courses of action;
counseling, or cooperatively advising with the client; and follow-
up, or carrying out the plan of action.

At about the same time, Carl Rogers was developing a
theory and method of counseling which culminated in the book,
Counseling and Psychotherapy in 1942. [10] The proposed method
sharply accentuated the already existing trend to client activity
and responsibility in the counseling interviews. Moreover, the
new approach challenged the clinical method as proposed by
Williamson and most other leaders in the vocational guidance
field in many major respects. Rogers stated that diagnosis was
unnecessary and even undesirable, that personal adjustment
was fundamental to vocational adjustment, that emotions and
attitudes perceived by the client were the crux of the counseling
process, that tests, inventories and personal data sheets were
not to be introduced unless the client so desired. The controversy was sharp and sometimes highly emotional, introducing
concepts of democracy and even ethics to justify the directive
or non-directive methods. As the shouts of battle began to sub-
side, around 1950, the counseling method was being subjected
to experimental scrutiny. The claimed advantages of one or
the other method were not demonstrated and Rogers himself
turned to other questions of apparently greater significance.

"Guidance" or "Counseling"?

As the year 1950 was approaching, the literature on vocational counseling was introducing more and more the concepts

of psychoanalysis. At this time, the word "guidance" had come into disrepute and was displaced by the term "counseling", in references to individual interviewing methods. The Division of Counseling and Guidance of the American Psychological Association changed its name, with little dissent, to the Division of Counseling Psychology. The change in name, for the most part, signified a general conviction that the most important phase in the efforts to bring about personal and vocational adjustment was counseling. The ferment in the entire field of guidance and counseling also involved opinions on the distinction, or lack of distinction, between counseling and psychotherapy. Some leaders in the field held that vocational counseling and psychotherapy should be skills practiced by the same person, while others claimed that there should be a real distinction between counseling psychology and clinical psychology, with the latter involved in psychotherapy. This controversy has been resolved in a practical way, but the theoretical difficulties in distinguishing precisely between guidance, counseling and psychotherapy still remain.

Interdisciplinary Approach

In trying to understand these trends in the half-century history of vocational counseling, I think it is helpful to call attention to a fundamental characterstic of the movement. From the beginning vocational guidance was imbedded in a practical philosophy, namely, that of helping the individual in an important and previously neglected phase of life. The guidance movement had a mission, a goal, but no scientific basis. It was eclectic and sought for and adopted new ideas and methods from all possible sources. Included were psychology, social work, occupational analysis, mental hygiene and industrial personnel work. With the increasing attention to, and apparent usefulness of psychoanalytic concepts, guidance and counseling seemed to find another fruitful avenue to understand individuals and to use concepts which accounted for vocational maladjustment in some clients.

Over the years, then, the emphasis in guidance changed from giving advice based on the training and experience by the counselor, to assisting clients in making choices and decisions.

Then, the mental hygiene movement made it clearer that vocational adjustment was one phase of overall adjustment to life, and highlighted the importance of counseling. And recently, the subconscious factors in adjustment seemed so important in determining vocational success that the principles of psychotherapy, especially from the field of psychoanalysis, somehow or other had to be incorporated in the theory and practice of vocationl counseling. [11]

Personality Factors in Vocational Counseling

In 1948, Friend and Haggard reported a study which illustrated the increasing emphasis in vocational counseling upon the emotional and attitudinal patterns formed in the early family history as related to job adjustment in adulthood. A group of men and women who came to a counseling center were divided into sub-groups with High and Low job adjustment. Clients with High job adjustment came from closely knit families, had shown much affection for their fathers, had resolved problems of rivalry with sisters and brothers in childhood, had been fairly happy in school, and had assumed their responsibilities with a sense of independence for their own lives. The group with Low job adjustment were more frequently family favorites, showed deep hostility toward their parents and siblings, had not outgrown the early pattern of family dependence, and were less able to accept supervision, or to assume easily the responsibility of supervisors or managers. Friend and Haggard explained the results as follows:

> The damaged self-confidence and anxiety which resulted from the inability to measure up (in the family situation) may be a strand in the link between an excess of this characteristic and a discordant work history. Moreover, the feverish striving to outdo others—a goal which is rarely reached—carries with it a deep sense of job dissatisfaction, as does the tension of constantly envying people in superior positions. (12, p. 48).

An example of the application of the concepts of dynamic psychology to industrial psychology, and more specifically, the selection of candidates for positions in top management is found in an article in the *Harvard Business Review,* on "The Executive Neurosis." [13] McMurray notes that persons may perform exceptionally well as assistants or as staff consultants rather than "line" management, and may consequently be given consideration for or placed in top executive posts. If such persons possess an essentially dependent character, due to unresolved oedipal conflicts, they may be unable to withstand the pressures inherent in making broad, top-level decisions. Their internal need for approval by dominant "father figures", and the ambivalence in dominance and submission, create such tensions as to diminish considerably their capacity for objective judgment. Such persons work interminable hours and seem to be immersed in their jobs and the company's welfare. However, the strong dependency needs and disguised hostility become full-blown in a prevalent form of "executive neurosis", with psychosomatic complaints, and impaired capacity for independent leadership.

Concepts such as these proposed by Friend and Haggard, and McMurray, are based upon the theory that unconscious personality factors have a substantial and predictable influence upon occupational choice. Vocational adjustment will depend upon whether the counselee chooses a field and type of work which fulfils his unconscious needs. Thus far, a theory of vocational counseling which incorporates such concepts of dynamic psychology has not been developed to the satisfaction of most leaders in the field.

If such a theory is developed in rich detail so as to be of proven value, the counselor must then determine how his insights should be brought to bear upon the counseling process. Unless the client can be assisted in understanding himself in terms of these needs, he is always subject to them. On the other hand, these needs cannot be brought to the person's attention in a short-term directive manner, because psychoanalytic theory teaches that he could not consciously "feel" their consequences and learn to control or modify them.

Implications of New Trends for Counselor Education and Practice

The perception that such deep-seated personality factors play an important role in the client's adjustment to work as well as the total scope of his life raises a nest of important issues to the vocational counselor. For example, how broad should his professional training be? How may he become skilled in identifying such basic patterns during the client's adolescent years when job choices are being made? Should these clients be referred for evaluation by the psychiatrist or clinical psychologist, or both? Have we reached a stage of progress that makes interdisciplinary practice an essential requirement? The short supply of counselors and other professional persons is a formidable practical hurdle, if we resolve the question in theory. How may the client's environment be modified in terms of working with parents, teachers, leaders of extracurricular activities, and other key figures in and out of school or work so that our insights may be used indirectly to the counselee's advantage? Or should we learn that part of our professional maturity consists in being able to appreciate our shortcomings without anxiety even while we know the client is heading for probable trouble? For, after all, his future destiny must be his own to work out, with our assistance being available to the extent that he chooses to use it.

Counselors' Future Needs and Attitudes

As we view the progress of the past fifty years, we see how increasingly complex the work of the vocational counselor has become. Although we have improved substantially many tools of our profession, new ones must be developed. Some of our critics have said that we are becoming too "ritualistic." We ask for better case histories, more psychological tests, a greater amount and quality of occupational information, more insightful counseling, curricular modifications in school and a wider variety of extracurricular experiences, closer contacts with the family, the counseling of parents as well as students, a larger number of teachers and others who know how to apply the principles of guidance in the context of their work, the utilization of an interdisciplinary approach, and constant follow-up with the counselees. Surely if our progress becomes fixed in shallow ritualistic activities, without a real appreciation of the value and inter-relationship of each phase to the goal of vocational adjustment for our students and clients, then we can hardly claim that advancement has been made.

On the other hand, if we are convinced that such complexity is part and parcel of a growing profession, the aims and values of which are proved, then our results will dissipate most of the criticism that will be leveled at us from time to time. The spirit of inquiry, practicality and objective application of our skills and knowledge are as essential today as in the early beginnings of the guidance movement. Above all, we are required to maintain a flexibility of outlook, an ever-increasing disposition to learn, and a continuing maturity of personality that will allay undue anxiety in ourselves, with greater benefit for our students and clients.

REFERENCE

(1) Borow, H. Milestones: A Chronology of Notable Events in the History of Vocational Guidance, pp. 45-66, in Borow, H. (Ed.) *Man in a World at Work*. Boston: Houghton Mifflin., 1964.

(2) Wrenn, C. G. *The Counselor in a Changing World*. Washington, D.C.: American Personnel and Guidance Assoc., 1962. pp. 173-4.

(3) Paterson, D. G. The Genesis of Modern Guidance. *Educational Record*, 1938, 19:36-46.

(4) Bordin, E.S., and Bixler, V.H. Test Selection: A Process of Counseling. *Educational and Psychological Measurement*, 1946, 6:361-374. Bixler, R.H., and Bixler, V.H. Test Interpretation in Vocational Counseling. *Educational and Psychology Measurement*. 1946, 6:145-155.

(5) Thorndike, E.L. *Prediction of Vocational Success*. New York: Commonwealth Fund, 1934.

(6) Latham, A.J. Job Appropriateness: A One-year Follow-up of High School Graduates. *Journal of Social Psychology*, 1951, 34:55-68.

(7) Anastasi, Anne. *Fields of Applied Psychology*. New York: McGraw-Hill Book Company, 1964, p. 450.

(8) Stone, C.H. Are Vocational Orientation Courses Worth Their Salt? *Educational and Psychological Measurements*, 1948,8:485-495.

(9) Brayfield, A.H. Putting Occupational Information Across. *Educational and Psychological Measurements,* 1948, 8:485-495.

(10) Rogers, C.R. Counseling and Psychotherapy, New York: Houghton Mifflin and Co., 1942.

(11) Wrenn, C.G. *The Counselor in a Changing World.* p. 56-57.

(12) Friend, J.G., and Haggard, E.A. Work Adjustment in Relation to Family Background. *Applied Psychology Monographs,* 1948, No. 16.

(13) McMurray, R. N. The Executive Neurosis. *Harvard Business Review,* 1952, 30:33-47.

HELPING YOUTH GET JOBS

ELI B. COHEN

Executive Secretary, National Committee on Employment of Youth

It is generally agreed that one aspect of the guidance counselor's work includes placement. Placement covers the academic or occupational activity in which youth are engaged after their high school graduation or separation. For some, this activity is college, for others employment or the services. The paper that follows is concerned with aiding the counselor in his assisting youths in their quest for employment.

The importance of the student's seeking employment is undoubted. And the counselor must regard his work in this area as the final test of his counseling efforts. All students, including the college bound, should be oriented towards jobs.

"Job readiness" should be determined concerning applicants for employment. People who cannot assume responsibility are risking an initial pattern of failure if they seek work. Elements of job readiness are the possession of a usable skill, motivation for work, physical fitness and emotional stability.

The job applicant must plan a campaign to sell his services. He must decide on one or more specific jobs in the light of his assets and skills. He must be able to prove his claimed abilities. He must learn where he should look for a job, usually the personnel department of a firm. Then he must plan out his approach to the employer. Should he write letters? Use the telephone? How should he obtain the face-to-face interview? What should he bring to the interview and how should he conduct himself during it? Should he have a job resume? How about the follow up to the interview? All these topics are discussed.

The counselor can help the student by working with him in all the above areas. In a special way, the counselor should review with the student his assets, skills and interview technique. To be of real help to students, the counselor must know the labor market and the problems of new workers.

Pre-employment counseling is a key to happiness for most people.

It is paradoxical that a staff member of the National Child Labor Committee, long concerned with keeping children out of the labor market, should present a paper about how to help youth get jobs. It is certainly a sign of the changing times. The exploitation of young children has been virtually ended, but simultaneously today's youngsters are being deprived of pre-work experiences and opportunities that would help prepare them more properly for work and adult life. Encouraging better preparation for work, more job opportunities, fuller public and community attention to youth employment problems has become a national necessity.

My topic is not about counseling techniques. I shall talk instead about the content of the pre-employment interview, about what is concerned in the discussion between the counselor and the counselee in the latter's search for employment. We shall address ourselves to such questions as: How to look for a job. Where to look. How to handle interviews with employers. How to get a job interview with an employer.

In these days of heavy emphasis on psychodynamics, mundane matters such as placement and employment and job opportunities tend to become step-children. In the pre-employment interview, for example, there is little room for using non-directive techniques. But actually, the pre-employment counseling interview is the payoff interview. This is the end result of all counseling. This is the interview that keeps counselors "honest." If we are not realistic and effective in counseling, there will be "a day of reckoning" when the counselee is not able to achieve the goal of finding a job in the occupation that we helped him select. [1]

Perhaps you feel this is not your concern if you are counseling only youngsters who are college bound. But even the college-bound youngster needs to be concerned with finding employment; many counselees will be seeking part-time or summer employment. Even if they do not need to earn money, work experience can be exceedingly valuable to them. It gives them an opportunity to be exposed to and explore various types of occupations. It helps in their development as adolescents when they take responsibility in a job. They need to relate to other people and to handle money; these are all factors, positive or negative, in adolescent development. If counselors help them get off to the right start in a job, they will help them avoid future scars in their job relations. To put it another way, the interview with the counselee about the job can frequently be his first contact with the world of work. It can set the pattern of how he will function in relation to the world of work for the rest of his lifetime.

An Illustration

A case in point is that of a young man, just under thirty, interested in changing jobs. When asked why he wanted to change jobs, he said, "I don't like my boss." In a period of about eight years, he had had five different jobs. In every case he didn't like the boss, a clear pattern of difficulty with his employers. He came from a broken home; his parents were divorced; he was married, but was having difficulty with his wife. His whole life history had been a pattern of perceived rejection by people he had been in contact with, particularly those who had been in a relationship of authority with him. Asked if he had seen a counselor at school, he first said no and then he said, "Yes, yes, I did. But it really wasn't very much." Since he was not going on to college, the counselor had not given him much attention, being more concerned with the college-bound students; here was a continuation of the pattern of rejection in his mind. This young man was looking for a father substitute in a boss to whom he would make overtures every time he went to a new job. And when he was rejected or appeared to be rejected, he immediately thought in terms of getting another job. His problem existed long before the school counselor saw him. But had this counselor been alert to his situation, and had the counselor helped him understand the differences between a parent and a boss, perhaps the counselor could have contributed to saving this young man a good deal of wear and tear through the ensuing years.

Job Readiness

If counselors are to deal with the business of employment, they need first to understand the concept of job readiness. Youth not thoroughly ready for employment, placed in the position of seeking work prematurely, risk a history of failure, not only in their future employment relationships but in all relationships. There is much we need to learn on how to determine job readiness; sometimes it's almost a matter of intuition. Perhaps the key word is "reality." And how real are the youngster's interest, desires, aspirations? How honest and real is the evaluation of his or her ability? Obviously, the youngster who seeks employment as an executive as his entry job is not ready.

A usable skill, not necessarily a highly developed skill, is another factor in job readiness. It will help if the youth can operate specific machines in an office or factory, but it is also suitable if he has the ability to handle relatively simple tasks such as following directions, finding his way around the city in running errands, and dealing with people in a retail store.

A third factor is a realistic purpose in wanting to work. Money is a very realistic purpose. Likewise experience would be a realistic purpose. But on the other hand, using work as an excuse for running away from school would be unrealistic. (Hardly unrealistic in this respect are the school dropouts from deprived neighborhoods where the schools are apparently incapable of meeting their educational needs.)

Fourthly, the youngster ought to be physically ready in terms of health, ability to handle tasks assigned within the required time. Finally he must be emotionally ready; for some this perhaps is the most important of all.

Illustrative of the latter is the case of a high school junior in the commercial course headed for dropout status before graduation. I offered her a part-time work experience at my office in the hope that it might build up her self-confidence and make her see the relationship between finishing school and getting a job. She accepted, but it was quite a problem. She could not work out in the open office because she was afraid that everybody was looking over her shoulder, seeing what she was doing. We placed her in a private office. She sat there for half an hour, emotionally frozen and immobilized. Her fingers couldn't work.

She finally came into me and said "Let's call it off. I can't do it."
She just was not emotionally ready.

Planning the Job Campaign

Assuming your counselee is ready for work, how should he
proceed? Looking for a job is a question of planning and then
executing the plan. Planning a job campaign takes careful, pains-
taking preparation. Most youngsters take a completely passive
approach. They will register at any agency, then go home, sit
by the telephone, and wait for the agency to call them. This
might have been appropriate in the days when there were plenty
of jobs to go around. Despite our current prosperity economy,
there just aren't enough jobs for all young people who want to
work. Therefore, a much more active approach to the problem
of finding a job is required today.

Looking for a job can be likened to a sales campaign. The
job-seeker is selling the most important thing he's got—himself.
He is the product. In planning a job campaign, he must define
his market, know who his customers are (his potential employers), and find a way of reaching and approaching them.
Look at the product in terms of what the youth has to offer an
employer, for no employer is going to hire just because the
youngster needs a job. The one who is going to be hired in a
competitive situation is the one who can convince the employer
that he can do something for him. It is important to decide on
one or more specific jobs to seek. Telling an employer that you
want or can do "anything" to an employer means "nothing."
The best way to select a job goal is to inventory what the youth
has to offer. Review and take into account such factors as interests, training, skills, ablilities, aptitudes, and physical assets.
Help the counselee add up these assets into a pattern of one
or more job objectives.

Beyond the job goal and assets, the counselee needs to back
up his job hunt with specific material and examples which will
demonstrate and justify his abilities to the employer. Wherever
possible, illustrate with actual results for the youth's efforts.

Where does one look for a job? It can't be done on a hit
or miss basis. Nor can you be effective by just knocking on a door
here and there. Pinpoint your target and develop your market.

Work up a list of prospective employers who can be approached. Which employers are approached will depend on what is sought. If employment is desired in a particular neighborhood, develop a list of employers in that area. Some youngsters have preferences with regard to size of company or the reputation of the company. Usually it is best to pick the employers in the industries that are most likely to hire for the job goal determined by the counselee. The names and addresses can be found in directories—telephone directories, industrial directories, etc. These can be found in any good library. It is best to locate the name of a specific individual in the company to approach. A letter or a phone call to a specific individual will get you further than an approach to the company in general. What individual in the company? Almost invariably the personnel department is thought of first. And often this makes the most sense. But consider also approaching the individual who would be the youth's superior if he is hired and who will make the ultimate hiring decision.

Contacting The Employer

Having helped the counselee determine what he has to offer and where to look, the next question is how to approach the employer most effectively. There are several ways. Sending out typewritten letters has many adherents. Letters are cold and impersonal, and of greatest value when there happens to be an opening at the time the letter is received. Otherwise, the chief value of a letter is in making contact with an employer when there has been no previous contact or no other entry to the company. The average executive has his "buffer state" in the form of a secretary and it may be hard to get him on a direct phone call. However, the letter, followed up by a phone call will help establish some identity on the part of the job-seeker. The second approach, as already mentioned, is the telephone call. It is not generally recommended unless there has been some previous introduction or contact with the employer, and then it is best used as a follow-up to a letter.

There are at least three more methods for reaching an employer with a job opening. One is to apply at the "gate;" i.e., at the plant or office of the company. This can be time-consuming and generally means an interview at the personnel department. Another method is to answer newspaper help-wanted advertisements. This has the advantage that an actual opening exists. A third method is working with employment agencies for referrals to job openings. Most employment agencies—except those specifically geared to youth—are more likely to be helpful to experienced adults.

Regardless of the method employed—and it is advisable to use a combination of several, or all—the objective is to obtain a face-to-face interview with the employer. Hiring is rarely done without one. In the interview, the applicant comes alive, can answer the employers questions, can sell himself. Introductions to employers from friends, neighbors and relatives can be exceedingly effective. The majority of people get jobs this way. [2]

Often it is very difficult to see an employer. He is a very busy man. One way to capture the employer's interest is the advice approach. Here the youngster gets in to see the employer on the basis that he would like the advice of an experienced executive. In addition to the intrinsic value of the executive's advice, this approach also has the advantage of getting the employer "on your side."

Preparing to be Interviewed

Now we come to the key question: how does the youngster prepare himself for the employer interview, present himself in the most favorable light, and thus get hired? First there is the necessity of learning as much as possible about the company. This will help in deciding whether it makes sense to work for the company. Knowing the company's reputation, status, and recent developments will also enable an applicant to talk more intelligently to the employer. He will have a sincere reason for wanting to work for the employer; he can be more persuasive in selling himself. Getting the information needed may be difficult. There are reports available about companies through stock market brokers or business magazines. The most reliable information often comes from somebody who knows the company, or who works there, or who may have worked there in the past.

Secondly, in preparing for the interview, the youngster should have certain facts and documents in order, such as a social security card or number, names and addresses of references, birth certificate or working papers, licenses, union cards, or military records. Those seeking work that involves a specific talent—art, for example—should bring along samples of their work. Most important is to have readily available the facts on one's self. The applicant should be sure, for example, to be able to list all previous employment, including name and address of employer, names of supervisors, duties, dates of employment and reason for leaving. Other data he should be ready to provide might include education, favorite school subjects, extra-curricular activities, age, etc.

On the Job Resume

Should the youngster have a resume when he goes for an interview? Resumes have become a great American institution. No one can go to an employment agency without being asked for one. Personally, I find resumes become a perpetuation of what the person has been doing all along. To try to break out of the straight and narrow of past jobs is most difficult because everything is focused on what you have done before. They tend to become a chronological history of the past rather than bringing out real values offered to a prospective employer.

But since youth inevitably will be asked to prepare resumes, it might be well to review what ought to go into one. The identifying information should be right at the top—name, address, and telephone number. Follow this with a statement of job objective, a concise description of the job desired. It helps to focus attention on his goal and it gets across to the employer the valuable message that he is a person who knows what you are looking for. Then summarize the background as it bears on the job objective. An applicant for a job as a typist, for example, would want to list her typing speed. Next should come either education or employment history. A youngster with a good deal of employment experience relevant to the job sought should list employment first. But one with relatively little employment or irrelevant jobs might put education first and then employment history. Finally, certain personal data should be listed, such as age, marital status, health, etc.

During and After the Interview

In the employer interview young people are much more assured when they recognize the importance of letting the employer do as much of the talking as possible. This pays off by getting more information and often creating a favorable impression. [3]

The key thing, in my opinion, in an interview with an employer is to find out what kind of a person and what qualifications the employer is looking for. Knowing what the employer wants, he can talk about himself in that image if he feels that you have the desired qualifications. In other words, the formula for success in selling himself into a job is to demonstrate that his qualifications match the employer's requirements and match them more so than anybody else who is applying for the job. But in order to be able to match them, he has to be sure that he knows what his qualifications are and he has to find out what the employer's requirements are. It helps to relax job interview tension by telling counselees to approach the interview as a survey in which they are going to find out what this employer wants. Avoid pressing the employer for a definite answer prematurely. If he is not ready to make up his mind about hiring the applicant at the time of the interview, he cannot give a positive answer. It is wise to emphasize the positive and to avoid the negative. Avoid especially any talk about your personal problems.

Follow up after the interview is important. A "thank you" note to the employer can work wonders. Many have gotten jobs as a result. The "thank you" letter serves both as an acknowledgment of the employer's courtesy and as a reminder of your conversation.

Back at the School or Agency

The pre-employment interview offers two challenges to the counselor. First is the challenge of really understanding the youngsters who are being counseled. These adolescents are striving for adulthood, but are simultaneously in conflict with their feelings of dependency. They want to work but they're afraid to work. They want to look for a job, but they're scared to death of talking to an employer. Thus the counselor needs

to know what's going on in the youth's mind and needs to prepare and reassure him for making these first approaches to the
outside world. Instead of pep talks, the counselor should point
out that these feelings are normal, that all youngsters go through
this experience. The counselor should review with the young
person what he has to offer in relation to this job so he can
develop the kind of confidence he needs in order to handle
these interviews.

The second challenge to the counselor is to learn about
jobs, employers and the labor market. It has become fashionable
for counselors to deal with the psyche whereas dealing with
job problems is beginning to be looked down upon. I believe
you are derelict in your responsibility if you do not strengthen
your knowledge and ability to handle job problems.

Examples of Errors in Counseling

Let me tell you about two cases where the counselors were
incompetent in the employment area with near disastrous consequences. A man in his forties was an insurance salesman. He
had been told by his counselor that he was very good at dealing
with people, and thus he became an insurance salesman. His
counselor did not know much about the occupation of selling
insurance. The one thing you need in selling insurance is a pretty thick skin. Although this is an occupation in which people
are really helped in providing their families against dependency,
the prevailing attitude in the community about insurance sales-
men is that they are a bunch of pests. People cross to the other
side of the street to avoid them. This was a very sensitive fellow
who was extremely hurt by a minor slight; he wanted to be
loved by all. If he had gone out of his way deliberately to pick
the job that he was least calculated to succeed in, he couldn't
have made a more accurate choice than insurance selling. Of
course, he was not making an adequate living in this work.

Another situation concerned a young man who was an engineer for one of America's largest corporations who wanted to
quit his job. He had been told to go into engineering. He sat
at a board all day long, drafting and designing, bored with his
dull technical job. Actually he was not interested in development work. After a number of counseling sessions, we both

agreed that he would be a good sales engineer. He liked to deal with people, and had enough of a flair for the technical to involve selling something of a technical nature. We also explored further his feelings about his employer and it became clear that he hated the company because he was unhappy in his work. He developed a plan to seek a transfer within the company where he might be a sales engineer. This he did successfully and the last time I heard from him he had been promoted to a management job. A counselor who knew enough to differentiate among various types of engineering occupations might have saved him much trouble.

These two young men had their entire lives disorganized because of their job problems. Not only were they unhappy at work, they were unhappy at home and with their families. And yet by helping them solve their job problems, we seemed to have touched the key which helped put everything else in place. As they made their job adjustment, the other adjustments followed.

Importance of Employment Counseling

Without trying to make any exaggerated claims for it, the field of employment counseling represents one of the keys to the adjustment of people. If employment counseling isn't properly handled, we can be lead into bad counseling generally and poor adjustment.

1. For material on practice of job interviews, cf. Hoppoch, R. *Occupational Information*. New York: McGraw-Hill, 1963, pp. 312-315, 446-456.

2. Super, D. E. *The Psychology of Careers*. NewYork: Harper and Brothers, 1957, p. 103.

3. Splaver, Sarah. *Your Career—If You're Not Going to College*. New York: Julian Messner, 1964, Chapter IV.

GROUP COUNSELING IN THE SCHOOLS

GORDON KLOPF

Associate Professor of Education
Bank Street College of Education

In explaining the nature of group counseling, Dr. Klopf points out that it provides the opportunity for learning which comes from the peer group, not from adults. He discusses some characteristics which would disqualify a person from becoming a group counselor, and he also notes the qualities which seem to be important for the successful group counselor. Certain kinds of knowledge and understanding seem to be indispensable for him. How the group is organized, the dynamics of the group process and some precautions for success are topics which are also sketched.

I would like to talk about the new technique we have been working with in the past couple of years, group counseling. First of all, group counseling has to be differentiated from group guidance and group therapy. You might say that group guidance includes the home room, the guidance class, the senior class assembly, the college night, or the career seminars, all highly structured. Now group therapy is used by the psychologist, the psychiatrist, or the psychoanalyst. They work with people who usually have deep seated personality problems and conflicts who are brought together in an institution, a doctor's office, a clinic or a hospital.

The Meaning of the Term

Group counseling is sort of in between the role of group guidance and group therapy. It is more in the direction of group

116

therapy. It is a technique and tool which can be used very effectively in both schools and colleges and even with elementary groups. It is a means of using the collective forces of the group in a staff structured situation to move toward greater self understanding, evolving plans of action and of testing new behavior. From seven to ten students are brought together in a school situation to help them to use the maximum interaction potential of the group to deal with some of life's problems.

Group counseling offers an opportunity for growth through the insight which comes from the peer group, not from the teacher or the counselor. As the students sit together in a group, the counselor is always there to ask questions which will test reality, and to develop interaction and to give support. The counselor in the group counseling situation maximizes the interaction of the group. Students with similar problems are urged to talk about them. They share insight and understanding. They may secure greater understanding because the counselor is not telling them, they are getting it from peer friends. They are dealing with problems together and this is quite different from sitting alone in the counselor's office.

At times I have been asked why I do not use the term "multiple counseling." In brief, I like the term group counseling. The term multiple counseling is confusing. It is different from group therapy and from group guidance. You begin with school problems, with school concerns. But this question often comes up, and it came up yesterday in a class. We had a fine report of some of the research being done in group counseling in Garden City. The question was asked, "You say you deal with attitudes, feelings, and values in counseling, but say it really goes deep into personality dynamics. How do you, the high school counselor, the college counselor handle it?"

First of all, your responsibility is not to do therapy. You should, if possible, make a referral if the person needs it. One thing I think you ought to be very careful of is closing up the child, like saying, "I think we ought not to talk about this here." You have to have some way to give him satisfaction. You have to, for the moment, deal with it. In group counseling you will find problems being expressed and brought to light which you did not know existed. Individual counseling and referrals frequently have to follow the first session for some of the group members.

Who Cannot Become Counselor to the Group

Now let us look more specifically at group counseling, who does it, and how you do it. First of all, I do not think that all counselors can do this effectively. I think it easier to teach or do group guidance, than to do group counseling. One counselor educator from the Middle West says that no one who has taught for more than five years can ever become an effective counselor. This instructional, telling pattern is so ingrained in the behavior of the teacher that he cannot shift gears at 28, or 35 to become a counselor. I believe that some people cannot ever become counselors and some can at fifty or sixty. It depends upon one's range of behavior, his flexibility, whether or not one wants to change and can change. I think there are certain types of individuals who can use a wide range of behaviors who work more effectvely in group counseling. The rather extensive action research project which we did this last year with a group of elementary and secondary school counselors in Garden City supports this conviction.

Who Can Become Counselor to the Group

First of all, the person who works with small groups in counseling has to be a non-hostile person. You say, but what teacher is hostile? Well, just visit the schools today and you see the hostility that some teachers and counselors have toward young people. If you get a good deal of satisfaction, and many people in education do, out of bossing, directing, out of "really telling people off," you are not going to be very effective in a group counseling situation.

To do group counseling, you have to be more on the "saintly" side, permissive, and accepting. You are providing a sanctuary for people, not a cell, or office of interrogation, which sometimes counseling or advising becomes. You have to be a person who tends to be one who emphasizes the positive rather than the negative, and not in a sentimental fashion. You look for the things that the students are saying and see in them potential for personality changes. You are able to capitalize on these with the observations you make. You have to be at ease and non-directive. A report on the counselors who went through the year long in-service training program for group counseling in Garden City found that the counselors who were too non-directive initially and had to develop more structure, at the end of the year had more response, more interaction and more discussion and insight coming from the peer group in the group counseling than the highly structured, instructional, aggressive, directive sort of counselor. However, we all have roles to play and it is interesting to note in this project in Garden City, that even the directive person with certain kinds of students is very effective in certain situations. However, in general I am convinced that non-directive behavior is the more effective.

As a professional person in group counseling you have to have a good deal of psychological understanding of people, you have to know personality dynamics, particularly of adolescents, or the age group with which you are working. If you are doing group counseling with the fourth or fifth grade, you have to know that the child operates in terms of the here and now, he does not have the perspective of time that you have with the sixteen or seventeen year old. Group counseling with college students again is quite different. There have been some very effective group counseling programs going on at Brooklyn College. At this level the students have more perspective on their behavior. The conversation is rich. However, the conversation with the fourth or fifth grade is related to play, to things right within their own world. The child lives closer to the here and now. You have to know the characteristics of human development, how youth behave at certain ages if you are going to help young people in group counseling.

You also have to have some knowledge of how groups develop and how people function in groups. What are the patterns of group behavior? First of all, you find a group is kind to a counselor. But a group will always test its leader shortly after the first or second session, and if this is threatening or disturbing you have to realize that groups do this. There are known ways in which the group of people who come together function as a group.

You must understand group structure and group development. You must know the skills of handling group discussion and how to guide the group through problem solving steps. To me, the most important skill that you have to have is being able to handle highly explosive situations quickly and at the right moment, knowing what to say at the right time. For example, if we are looking in on a group and there is interaction going on between Jane and Thomas with an argument developing, do you, the counselor, enter at this moment or do you wait five minutes? Now maybe after five minutes, there is another topic going on and it will be too late. In individual counseling the counselor has time to think. Time and momentary insight are not as important. But in group work, you have to have the skill, the insight at the moment to know what to do. If you do not enter at that moment, the situation is lost. In counseling you can sit there, you can smoke, you can twiddle your pencil and think, "Now, how am I going to answer this, how will I deal with this?" A group counselor cannot have this opportunity. You cannot have this little conversation with yourself. You have to act then and now, or the interaction of the moment may be lost.

Assembling the Group

Now let us look at the group in group counseling. First, the group size should be about from seven to ten. Some social psychologists tell us that we can never really relate to more than about seven people; that the moment you get more than ten, eleven, or twelve, you have two groups developing. When you have too large a group, you get a second basic interaction pattern. We want to keep one interaction pattern, keep this group interacting among itself. I say seven to ten because you may find one or two leaving the group.

The issue is always, how do you bring a group together? Our experience during the last couple of years, shows that you bring them together with a mutual concern, at least an initial mutual concern. What are some of these we have been dealing with? A common one is underachievement. You will find that they come together with similar problems, for example, all seventh graders, or tenth graders, who had three failures the previous semester. They appear to themselves to be "in the same boat." This is a very important element in the early history of the group in group counseling. The student is given a complete clarification as to why he is invited to join the group.

You tell them honestly what the concern is. The group may move faster if it knows what the problem is to begin with, if it is clear why they are there.

You need to have a selection interview with each one you are considering. During the interview you give each of them an orientation to the purpose of the group. You have to clarify certain limitations and expectations. One is that they "buy" the experience for about seven or eight sessions. The group for the first two or three sessions may not have any meaning for the student. If he is with it for seven or eight, it is more likely to have meaning. So he tries it for six, seven or eight sessions. Secondly, he agrees to participate, as much as possible to share, to talk in the group. He realizes that he has some responsibility for the group, that as much as possible, he has to contribute. In some groups with acting out boys, for example, we make other conditions. They cannot fight and they cannot leave the room. However, they can use their own language, they can walk around the room. So, depending upon what the situation is, you will set your expectations to meet the needs of that particular group. With some junior high school students it is important to have the policy that one cannot talk at the same time that someone else is talking.

The Group Counseling Process

Let us look now for a few minutes at the process, what you do in group counseling. How does a group move along? At the first session it is important to reemphasize what the goals are, what the expectations are. You operate very permissively initially. How the group perceives you initially lasts a long time. If you are going to do group counseling, be more unstructured than structured or the children will think you are going to be running all the sessions and that you are going to play the same teacher role as you have done in the classroom or in group guidance. There is always a way to get young people in a group to introduce themselves, particularly when they do not know each other. You might begin by introducing yourself, you might ask them to introduce themselves. I think the technique of going around the group is not a good one, for then they sometimes think that they always have to make comments in order around the circle. You have to kind of sense your opening session. You may not get all the children introduced but they will soon learn all of the names.

Initially in group counseling we permit a lot of ventilating. By ventilating, I mean you let the child, for instance in an underachieving group, just pour out his feelings and experiences as he percieves them or wants to relate them. Then you move from ventilating to some real problem solving or looking back at this behavior, reality testing.

If you are working with a group long enough, you also let them test some new behaviors. One of the groups we had in the city this last fall, broke some of the furniture in the first session. They were highly aggressive, acting out boys. They still talk and throw a few things, but they have learned new behaviors and they can relate to one another for forty-five minutes, without too much poking or fighting. They learned some new controls in this group situation with a counselor who has set certain limitations but who also has been very understanding of them, in quite different ways than that of the teachers, the policemen, or the parents. Some of the new behaviors they have experimented with may transfer to the classroom and to other group situations in their life.

Some Precautions

If you are going to experiment with group counseling, tape your sessions, listen to your own tapes, and get someone else in your school to listen. If possible, have someone with professional experience to comment on your tapes and to work with you for a time. One of my very good students, one very able young man, a fine teacher with a good experience and background, had a whole semester of theoretical training, but except in role playing he did not work with a real group. What did he do the first session in his own group? He gave a ten minute talk on self concept, to eleventh graders. He listened to his tape. He was embarrassed, shocked. Then he reverted to a very passive, unstructured behavior. His group did come around, and he finally had a very effective relationship with his group. He said even at the time when he was giving the speech on self concept, it just came forth. "I didn't know I was doing it until I listened to the tape, I didn't know how I behaved in the group."

An additional precaution is directed towards preventing the group from splitting up into several factions. Towards that end, we guard against personal interviews with members of a group, particularly with adolescents. The group therapist will as a rule not carry on extensive therapy with an individual who is also in a group at the same time having group counseling sessions. If I am meeting with a group of students, and I am meeting three of you individually, there is quite a difference not only in the interaction pattern among the three I know well and the others I do not know so well. For instance, the person I am meeting individually may say in the group, "Well, Dr. Klopf, I told you about that the other night in our discussion, and I do not want to say it here." Well, this may ruin the group dynamics. Now it is true that if one girl wants to know about nursing and no one else has this need, you can say, "Drop into the guidance office sometime when it is convenient for you and we'll give you the booklet on nursing and talk to you about it." But this is quite different from carrying on a series of interviews with the members of your group individually at the same time that you are seeing them as a group.

Conclusion

I would like to conclude with some favorite lines of mine which sum up the importance of the potential of our human relationships:

> No man is an island entire of itself.
> Every man is a piece of the continent, apart of the main.
> Any man's death diminishes me
> Because I am involved in mankind
> And therefore never send knoll for whom the bell tolls
> It tolls for thee.

We all share in the other's destiny. Can we help young people to realize this? Do we use the potential of groups, of human relationships, to help young people to help themselves?

For Further Reading

Gordon, T. *Group-Centered Leadership*. New York: Houghton Mifflin Company, 1955.

Klopf, G. (et al.) *Interns in Guidance*. New York: Bureau of Publications, Teachers College, Columbia University, 1963.

Mathewson, R. H. *Guidance Policy and Practice* (3rd. ed.) New York: Harper, 1962.

National Society for the Study of Education. (Edited by N. S. Henry). *Personnel Services in Education*. Fifty-Eighth Yearbook. Chicago: University of Chicago Press, 1959.

Symonds, P. M. *What Education Has to Learn From Psychology*. New York: Bureau of Publications, Teachers College, Columbia University, 1958.

Taylor, H. The Philosophical Foundations of General Education. National Society for the Study of Education. *General Education*. Fifty-first Yearbook, Part I. Chicago: The University of Chicago Press, 1952.

Warters, Jane. *Group Guidance Principles and Practice*. New York: McGraw-Hill Book Company, 1960.

WHAT THE HIGH SCHOOL COUNSELOR SHOULD KNOW ABOUT STUDENT PERSONNEL AT THE COLLEGE LEVEL

REV. VICTOR R. YANITELLI, S.J.

President, St. Peter's College

Counselors at the college level and those at the high school level both agree that it is important that they have a good knowledge of their fellow counselor at the other level. Too little is done in practice to achieve this knowledge and understanding. Father Yanitelli provides help in one aspect of this communication problem.

After describing the situation of the freshman in college, the advantage of adequate educational planning in the college is indicated. The educational and attitudinal atmosphere of the college can be learned. Methods of obtaining this information are suggested. As a part of the college picture, the exact role of the student personnel program should be studied. Student government, the athletic program and the extracurriculum are cited as examples for scrutiny. The counselor may help his students to compare their requirements with the complete picture of the college.

My text is taken from Dean Whitla of Harvard. It is really the quote of a quote from an article wherein Whitla [1] draws from the Harvard experience to show that the large university college environment is nearly always defined by the newly arrived student in terms of coldness and isolation. The experience is almost endemic to freshmen everywhere and it leads us up to one of the basic presuppositions that all of us who are in the business of student personnel must understand. To make the point clear, Dean Whitla cites a passage from Richard Hughes' *The Fox in the Attic*:

After all, it is only grown men who think of school as a microcosm, a preparation for adult life: to most boys at any time school *is*
life, is itself the cosmos: a rope in the air you will climb, higher,
and—then, quite vanish into somewhere incomprehensible anyhow. [2]

College life is for the student the microcosm. College life is
his world.

He moves in that world experiencing all the inner drives,
the confusions, the impatiences and the frustrations that
accompany his own concept of what his adulthood should be.
His post-adolescence is alive with the desire and the half-
understood craving for independence and self-reliance. His
needs demand an environment in which growth can be promoted. Where the need is great, much will depend on the
college counselor's work in creating what Carl Rogers has termed
"The Interpersonal Relationship: the Core of Guidance." [3]
Rogers requires of the college counselor first of all congruence,
meaning that the counselor has to be what he *is* without front
facade. Secondly, the counselor must have empathy, that is,
the understanding of the client's private world, a positive regard
for the client which is unconditionally total and therefore free
of the value judgments which might influence or form the
basis of the interpersonal relationship. The value judgments
may be there, but they can never be the basis for a proper
interpersonal relationship in the guidance situation.

Freshmen in College Guidance

It may seem strange that in a paper directed to the high
school counselor, the introduction should be exclusively concerned with the student and with the college counselor. This
apparent reversal of order is intended simply to highlight the
very real problem existing in institutions with an appreciably
large student body. On the one hand, the student comes to
college with the loneliness of the long distance runner and
frequently enough, in need of guidance. On the other hand,
guidance at its professionally highest level, requires an interpersonal relationship. The development of the interpersonal
relationship takes time and cannot be achieved in a single
interview. Consequently, the sheer force of numbers will prevent the guidance staff from counseling any more than a

rather generous handful of the multitude. Hence the problem of the high school counselor takes on a new magnitude in assisting the student to make his choice of college.

Dana L. Farnsworth, probably the most enlightened psychotherapist in the field of student mental health today, has provided good direction for the high school counselor to follow in order to escape the dilemma. Dr. Farnsworth [4] conceives the institution itself as an educational instrument with its own built-in type of guidance that is adequate for the greater majority of students who are not emotionally ill. The educational planning of the institution, as he sees it, cannot stop at how or what material is going to be presented to the students:

> It is my thesis that if the educational plannng is good and if careful and continuous thought is given to relations between faculty members and students, fewer students will become emotionally disturbed, and fewer will fail than if planning is devoted only to how and what material should be presented to students.... Not until students sense something of the character, ability, and basic friendliness of their teachers do they begin noticeably to respond, either in approval of an atmosphere conducive to learning or disillusionment at being caught in a trap. [5]

The High School Counselor Studies A College

The high school counselor's primary task—and perhaps this is his most difficult one—is to acquire by whatever means possible an intimate knowledge of the institution he is discussing with his client. Written material does provide factual information. He must learn all the facts available. Sometimes the catalogue can even give some evidence of the emotional climate of the institution. The real task however is to know the environment of student life at the institution. This can never be put down in writing. It has to be lived. And because the student personnel program is so intrinsically involved in every aspect of the student's life outside the classroom, a knowledge of the institution's student personnel services will contribute a great deal to the understanding of the institution's intangibles, the atmosphere and the spirit of the place.

At this point, the counselor may well find himself in a cul-de-sac,—and one constructed by the author at that. How does

one come to know "the institution's intangibles, the atmosphere
and the spirit of the place?" This is indeed a legitimate question.
Regrettably there is no simple answer, no skill or how-to-do it
technique to solve the problem. What the counselor needs here
in addition to the wisdom gathered through his own experience,
is a kind of art, an ability to probe intellectually beyond the data
of the senses to the motivating influences, the hierarchy of values
and the inner dynamics of the idea that makes the college what
it is, that gives it its real life and vitality.

This necessarily sounds vague but it merely signifies the
ability to take all the available materials and from their analysis
arrive at the reality they reflect. In a sense, the counselor will
act here like the doctor who cannot be satisfied with the meaning of symptoms until he has reached to their source. For
example, the catalogue—an instrument admittedly devised to
show the institution in its best possible light—could well be
supplemented with a subscription to the student newspaper.
For the student newspaper is an almost infallible index of
student concerns. Three or at most four editions would suffice
to get a fairly accurate picture of what the students consider
to be important; whether they are also involved in larger issues
of education, history and life or are hermetically enclosed in the
picayune contest between cliques. The same can be said of
the literary publication(s): the pseudo-aesthetic straining for
literary effect can be judged in an issue or two, as can the
solid striving for a mastery of expression. The admissions and/or
recruiting officer of most institutions will make these journals
available on request.

More helpful perhaps, and more revealing is the session
arranged with graduates of the counselor's high school now
attending the college in question. It is preferable by far to
bring in upperclassmen wherever possible, since college freshmen normally have yet to experience a whole year at the
institution. These sessions should be structured so that the
home-coming graduate may speak freely. Questions should be
carefully prepared in advance—if possible, they should be
based on items selected from the student newspaper—from
which the graduate will reflect his feelings on what goes on
in the college student life. Which are the major student power
blocs? How great a part does politics play in student activities?

Does student government look to the welfare of the student body as a whole? What kind of intellectual rapport exists between students and faculty? The answers to these and similar questions will open up a window on the true sentiments of the returning high school graduate and provide another source of information to be added to the counselor's store.

Finally, contact with the deans of men, deans of women, housing directors, directors of the campus center or college union, directors of student personnel, all those whose knowledge supplements the information given by the admissions officer, can be particularly helpful in the case of colleges that are not too well known to the counselor. The National Association of Student Personnel Administrators with secretarial headquarters at the University of Illinois in Urbana, will provide informational sources of contact with practically any institution from coast to coast. The counselor will find here a resource in terms of a person or persons whose whole preoccupation is with student life, whose existence is justified only according to the effort to make the student's growth whole and integrated with the institution's goals. The acquaintance with student personnel staff, when added to that acquired from student publications and from direct contact with the student experience, will provide a confluence and a congruence of evidence that points more than circumstantially to 'the atmosphere and the spirit of the place."

Student Personnel Services at the College

It helps to know what the institution means by student personnel and what image the college student personnel has of itself. Student personnel services, or the student personnel program, if you will, is guidance in a larger sense. Technical guidance by professionally qualified people forms a part of it, but in the broader meaning of the term, everything about student personnel relates to some kind of built-in guidance. A great deal can be learned about an institution if the institution could itself tell one—and often enough it cannot—just what its own hierarchy of values is in relation to the realm of student personnel.

Hopefully, everything in student personnel at institution X will be carefully thought out at least to the point where it manifests some noticeable reference—even indirect—to the institution's aims and objectives. This information will be important to you. Student personnel services must be intrinsically involved in the institution's whole educational process. If it is not, then one can only conclude that the student personnel program is nothing more than supervised fun and games. The only guiding purpose of student life and student activity may be negative (keep the students out of trouble, don't get the president upset, don't let anything ever be said or done or remarked except what is good, healthy, pious and edifying); this will tell you a lot about the institution as a whole, and whether your client needs that kind of environment. The first duty of the school counselor is to learn as much as possible about the institutional philosophy motivating its student personnel operation.

And the first question to be asked is how the student personnel program relates to education. What for instance, does housing mean at the institution? Is the student residence no more than a place of lodging, a cross between a hotel and a reformatory? Do food services mean feeding with a minimum of complaint—because everybody, even religious, complain about institutional feeding? Is the disciplinary function simply a police operation? Or has this thought been evolved with the students rather than for and at them? Has thought been given to the educational values of the social graces, courtesy, for instance, and cleanliness? If the institution has given some thought to these questions—whether successfully or not—it is an institution worth looking into because its motivating ideas are positive rather than negative.

The program begins with admissions. It is here that the process of fitting the student to the institution begins. It is really the first step in the orientation program. It is also the step with which the school counselor is most familiar. Knowledge of it is essential for any kind of communication with the person looking to higher education. It would be well to examine how the admissions officers use the knowledge derived from test scores, high school records and personal interviews. Take a second look if all three are duly considered and weighed together before coming to a final conclusion about the student's admissibility. The same approach to the office of the registrar should also provide insights as to what the institution does about its records, its stand on confidentiality and whether the information on the individual student is scattered or centralized.

The counseling—and/or psychological services—is particularly pertinent to your purposes. It pays to take the time to discover whether the educational and academic counseling begins with the faculty, or is left to the professionals alone. Does the faculty consider educational counseling as a routine part of their teaching? The answer to this question would seem to have greater meaning in the light of the fact that educational and academic problems originate for the most part, if not entirely, in the classroom. If academic advisement on the part of the faculty does exist, the next phase to investigate is whether this type of counseling is done in a vacuum or with some relationship of referral to the professional guidance services. Finally,—if the institution is Catholic—find out whether academic advisement and professional guidance are related in any way to the spiritual direction, the chaplains and religious counselors. Do all three phases of the guidance program know and make use of health services, remedial reading and study skills services, when and if these are present?

Student Life

The school counselor ought to inform himself about student life at the institution. What really is the student government there? Any student group organized simply to take orders from the dean is not really a student government. If your client is coming into the age where he has begun to push for independence, for self-reliance, and will soon make the overwhelming discovery that he can think, it would be well for the school counselor to know what type of student life will best fit his client. It would be a serious error on the part of the institution to make a pretense of student government. The intelligent young student will not be long in discovering the reality and the discovery will leave him disgruntled and disillusioned.

Be informed about the athletic program. This is particularly necessary in the case of healthy young men. They are coming up to college full of biological energy and if there is not some release provided through an intramural or a physical education program, the institution is going to pay for the absence of out-let in other areas of student interest. Intercollegiate athletics may have an educational value for a small number of partici-pants. Its greatest value to the mass of students lies in its function as rallying point for student enthusiasm. However, the student in a larger institution is, more often than not, far too sophisticated to be content with a losing team. Sometimes, it is impossible to get a winning team without becoming educationally corrupt. There is nothing particularly pure in having no scholarships for athletes, nor is there anything particularly sinful in hiring players to put on the weekly spectacle. Something is radically wrong however, when an educational institution says one thing in its catalogue and then does another in recruiting the best available athletic beef. If inter-collegiate athletics were not involved in money-making, if they had not become a kind of public possession of those who are entertained by it, there would be no problem in athletics today. The intention here has not been to give a disquisition on athletics but rather to indicate the value of information about the athletic program for the school counselor.

As for the student personnel program as a whole, the school counselor might well look for a statement from the institution, one that does more than just describe its services and activities. Look rather for a statement that might possibly reveal the attitude of the institution toward its own program. Have the student personnel services and activities been accepted by the entire academic community? By faculty? By administra-tion? Is there some sort of consensus about the place of student personnel and has an effort been made to integrate the student personnel program with all the other programs of the institution? If some endeavor at integration does not exist, the school counselor can almost certainly conclude that the personnel program is peripheral to the real educational intent of the institution. The fact of student activity and of student life in such an environment is almost certainly looked upon as little more than a necessary evil.

Information on the integration of the student personnel program with the other programs of the institution ought rightly to be followed by information on the coordination of the student personnel functions with one another. The internal aspect of this phase of student personnel is possibly even more than the institution's attitude on student personnel. It would seem that nothing would be more ineffective than to have an institutional approach of basic encouragement to student personnel program which is desultory, dispirited and internally uncoordinated.

The Extracurriculum

Frederick Rudolph's *The American College and University, a History,* [6] makes a startlingly clear point about the effectiveness of the student extracurriculum. By chapter and verse, his history shows how the students re-defined the nature of the American college in the extracurriculum. For instance, the college library was nothing,—or very little more than a collection of pious tracts—until the literary societies started to buy their own books. As far back as 1840 the societies at Williams possessed 10,000 volumes on science, literature, politics and philosophy; the 6,000 volumes of the University of North Carolina's literary groups was the best collection in the state; Bowdoin's 5000 to 6000 volumes, Brown's 3000, all were superior to the college library's collection. [7] The same impact was felt by the colleges when the fraternities replaced the literary societies. And of course, the rise of football began in fun outside the classroom and developed into the multi-million dollar entertainment of today.

The extracurriculum has received a new intellectual and a new social-minded emphasis from the post World War II era which has brought students into the field of civil rights, picketing, demonstrations in society. The question of student rights and above all, of student freedoms presses upon institutional administration everywhere. Nor is there any escape. It is a fact of life with which the institution and its administration must live. Peer group pressures seem to be greater upon the student more now than ever before, simply because they are more intense, more focused than ever before. The need for higher education as a requirement for starting anywhere in business or the professions, the increased competition, all combine to put pressures upon the student. Parents are registering their children for Harvard as far back as the primary school. The National Institute of Health cheerfully predicts that one out of every twelve Americans is going to undergo some kind of mental health problem in the next decade. And no increase of staff in psychological services will ever adequately cover the total needs of the students in our institutions. It therefore becomes crucial that the school counselor investigate what the institution itself is providing for the needs of the mass of its students. The student cannot learn too soon to be a self-starter. The institutional program servicing the group has become increasingly important to the individual student.

The Urban vs. the Rural College

A look into the problems confronting an urban institution as opposed to a rural institution is also a must for the school counselor. The life of the urban institution is open to every distraction and to every temptation. On the one hand, the student with the price of admission is more likely to attend a professional concert at Carnegie Hall than to listen to a pianist brought on campus to keep the young men home at night. The sports-minded seem to prefer the professionals to a losing team at home. On the other hand, the incipient beatnik who craves the Greenwhich Village atmosphere will gravitate to it,—nor are there enough policemen on campus to prevent him if he really wants to go. The school counselor must evaluate the student's competence and responsibility to himself, not for purposes of over-protection and spoon-feeding, but rather to weigh the student's chances for growth in such an environment. Something of the social and economic level of the institution should also come under consideration. Of course a good mixture of different degrees of these elements is healthy in a college. But the counselor should make sure that the student is not put in the position of being an intellectual, competent to stand up with the best brains of the student body but without the financial resources to spend as the others do. This could become tragic. It could turn the intellectually qualified student into a social misfit. In a certain sense, the same could be said of the religious groupings, especially in non-sectarian institutions, where the religiously committed student could find himself forced to make a choice between his companions and his faith.

The Individual and the College

Perhaps the overriding consideration should be to see just how much the institution suits its entire program to the students it admits. As counselor, you should compare your student to that program. This is about the most a human being can do at this particular stage of guidance in helping a student move from high school up to the college level. The principle to be followed is the old one that the insight is useless unless it comes from or is interiorly possessed by the client. Our guidance has meaning only in so far as it helps the client help himself, i.e., become more confidently self-directed. To this end Dean Whitla quotes Ralph Waldo Emerson:

> Although this garrulity of advising is born with us, I confess that life is rather a subject of wonder, than of dialectics.... We accompany the youth with sympathy, and manifold old sayings of the wise, to the gate of the arena, but 'tis certain that not by strength of ours, or of the old sayings, but only on strength of his own, unknown to us or to any, he must stand or fall. That by which a man conquers in any passage, is a profound secret to every other being in the world, and it is only as he turns his back on us and on all men, and draws on this most private wisdom that any good can come to him. [8]

This after all, is the goal of all our attempts to understand and guide the young toward adulthood,—the worthy goal of helping each person to come into his own strength, into the profound secret of his own, unique resources, the ultimate reason why the school counselor should know something about student personnel at the college level.

REFERENCES

1. Whitla, K., Guidance in the University Setting. *Harvard Educational Review*, XXXII (1962), 450-462.

2. Hughes, R., *The Fox in the Attic*. New York: Harper, 1961, p. 110.

3. Rogers, C., The Interpersonal Relationship: The Core of Guidance. *Harvard Educational Review*, XXXII (1962), 416-429.

4. Farnsworth, D. L., Who Really Helps Our Students? in *Personality Factors on the College Campus*. The Hogg Foundation for Mental Health, The University of Texas, 1962, pp. 93-110.

5. *Ibid.*, p. 94.

6. Rudolph, F. *The American College and University*. New York: Knopf, 1962, pp. 136-155, 373-393.

7. *Ibid.*, p. 143.

8. Emerson, R.W., The Conduct of Life, in *The Works of Ralph Waldo Emerson: Four Volumes in One*, New York, Tudor, n.d., pp. 161-162.

THE ROLE OF THE
SPIRITUAL COUNSELOR IN THE
HANDLING OF ADJUSTMENT PROBLEMS

LIONEL V. CARRON, S.J.

*Counselor, Psychological Service Center,
University of Detroit*

Throughout the high schools and colleges of the country it happens every year that individuals are assigned to the position of spiritual counselor. Some have been trained for the position, some have not. No matter what his background, if he works in this area or in any area of counseling, he should profit from reading Fr. Carron's analysis and experience.

Some religious counselors function as school chaplains and others are truly counselors in that they work with students who have personal problems which are based on religious sources. The paper concerns the latter type of counselor.

The role of the non-directive or client centered apporach in the religious counselor's work is discussed. Acceptance and permissiveness is viewed as extended towards the person and the emotions of the person, not necessarily toward all his actions. The atmosphere for counseling must be non-authoritarian, permissive and acceptant. It may be that the counselor will find it necessary to refer his counselees elsewhere and so he must have a good knowledge of local agencies and specialists to whom he can send some of his counselees.

There is a place for testing on the part of the religious counselor if he is trained in their use. Some tests require much training, others require little. The values of administering one of the latter type, the Mooney Problem Check List, are discussed.

Some readers will like the distinction between religious advising and religious counseling. The former is "authoritarian and directive... a form of teaching." The latter is "non-authoritarian, permissive and non-directive."

The practice of dividing counseling activities into separate areas and assigning these areas to different individuals is, of course, quite unnatural. The person counseled is a unity, a complex but integrated unity. His activities interact upon each other and commingle in many intricate ways. Spiritual exercises, psychological reactions, physiological functioning, vocational aspirations, educational activities, and intellectual operations do not take place in different parts of the individual but the whole person acts in the production of each activity. Strictly speaking, then, we cannot have different counselors who deal exclusively with psychological problems, or spiritual problems, or school problems, or vocational problems. The spiritual counselor, the school counselor, the vocational counselor, or the psychological counselor, though his primary function may be to deal with problems in a particular area of human activity, must nevertheless be cognizant of and deal with the whole person of his counselee, must be aware of and regard his physical and mental health, his intellectual powers, his previous training and experience. It is the whole Jerry Jones with all his abilities and disabilities, his assets and liabilities that he must help in his spiritual and religious deveopment. We believe that this principle cannot be overemphasized. In these days of departmentalism it is easy to lose sight of it.

There is another point which should be emphasized. That is this. In this paper we are restricting the term "Spiritual Counselor" to its proper and special meaning. In many schools and colleges the spiritual counselor is responsible for all the activities which are necessary and helpful in the spiritual life and growth of the school and college. In a Catholic college he arranges for daily Mass for the students. He provides ample opportunities for the students to go to confession and to receive Holy Communion at their reasonable convenience. He arranges for and supervises the annual retreats.

Besides these group activities there are certain individual activities that are the concern of the spiritual counselor, for example, advising students about adopting specific religious practices, such as meditation and daily examination of conscience, giving the information about the sodality, the missions, the priesthood and religious orders, encouraging them to participate in the various charitable and apostolic endeavors.

The Religious Counselor and Adjustment Problems

These group and individual activities, important as they are, are not our primary concern in this paper. Rather our concern is the role of the spiritual counselor in the handling of adjustment problems. And we would like to amend and interpret this statement as follows: the role of the spiritual counselor in helping the student to handle his adjustment problems, to help him understand and solve his spiritual and moral difficulties.

This brings us to the use of the word, "counsel," in its more restricted and proper sense, namely, an acquired virtue or habit by which a person comes to an understanding of his perplexities and as a result, can control and redirect his emotional reactions so that he arrives at a reasonable and effective solution of his adjustment problems.

This idea that counsel is a habit acquired by the individual and not something given him by the counselor is *implicit* in Carl Rogers'[1] advocacy of non-directive counseling and *very explicit* in Father Charles Curran's development of the same.

Father Curran holds that counseling in its strict sense must be non-directive and defines it as a:

> definite relationship where, through the counselor's sensitive understanding and skillful responses, a person objectively surveys the past and present factors which enter into his personal confusions and conflicts, and at the same time *reorganizes his emotional reactions* so that he not only *chooses better ways* to reach his reasonable goals, but also has *sufficient confidence, courage* and *moderation to act on these choices*.[2] (italics added)

As you know, Carl Rogers', and later Father Curran's, advocacy of non-directive counseling has resulted in some criticism. Especially in the field of religious and moral counseling has the idea of non-directive counseling been assailed as being dangerous to faith and morals. It is argued that the attitude of acceptance and permissiveness of the non-directive counselor can easily be taken in spiritual and moral counseling as an approval of something expressed by the counselee which is actually irreligious or immoral. That this is not true becomes evident from further consideration of the permissive relationship. In reality this relationship is not permissive unless the client feels that the counselor neither approves nor disapproves what he says. Moreover, it is not the irreligious or immoral act which is accepted or permitted by the counselor but the emotional attitude and expression of the counselee. With the expression of his repressed antagonisms and hostilities (even toward the counselor) he comes to understand his religious or moral perplexities and this insight will carry over into behavior that is religiously and morally mature. This, we believe, answers the objection that permissive counseling may give approval to ideas that are actually irreligious or immoral. If, however, the counselor feels that in dealing with religious and moral problems, he cannot be entirely nondirective, I ask him if he cannot be as non-authoritarian and permissive as possible.

This does not mean that, in our guidance work other than counseling in its restricted sense, we may not give authoritative information or advice and do authoritative teaching and training. Those are very necessary and important in our guidance activities. They are, however, directive activities originating in the adviser or instructor, and not in the students, and satisfy particular student needs at particular times. Far more important is it that the sudent's more fundamenal and universal need of growth in self-direction and self-integration be fostered by helping him in developing the habit or virtue of counsel. This can be accomplished if the counselor provides an atmosphere that is non-authoritative, permissive and acceptant.

At the beginning of this paper we ventured to say that our practice of dividing counseling activities into different areas of spiritual problems, vocational problems, psychological problems and assigning them to different counselors is quite unnatural. This has been verified by the extensive study that Father Curran made of the personality factors in counseling. As one of his conclusions he mentions the following:

> Nondirective therapy reveals powers within the personality itself which are productive of its own adjustment. This flows directly from the understanding that the personality as a whole is involved in every maladjustment. Even when there are difficulties for which medication and even surgery are necessary, when certain en-

vironmental changes are needed, or when definite instructions have to be given the client because of the knowledge he lacks, the process of adjustment is still essentially dependent on the part the person himself plays in reorganizing his own outlook. Unless the total personality is affected, the treatment of symptoms, physical or psychological, may cure the symptoms but have no lasting effect on the personality maladjustment. [3]

Principles, Not Cases

Some of you may be disappointed that we have confined the discussion to principles and general methods of counseling and have not discussed individual cases. Someone might stand up and say: "When are you going to stop talkng on about general principles and techniques of counseling and get down to the tough specific cases that haunt the spiritual counselor's office: the girl who pilfers, or is pregnant, or tells dramatic lies about herself or her family; the boy who periodically runs away from a good home, or has scruples or masturbates; the youngster who questions his faith or is losing it, who cannot keep away from a gang of hoodlums, who drinks too much or is starting to take dope, or, worst of all, believes he has a divine call to reform his family, his parish or his school."

May we answer this, first of all, by asserting that the principles and general methods that we have been discussing are practical and can be applied in individual cases. [4] You will not find that the application is automatic but through persistent and critical practice you will become expert in applying these methods to your individual students. The specific cases of other counselees, on the other hand, are isolated instances of particular applications of principles and methods. I believe that the case method is of little value in deciding actual cases that are always different from the one used as an example.

The Team Approach

May we also answer this objection to our discussion of general principles rather than specific instances by citing some of our experiences at the University of Detroit? We have a full-time spiritual counselor and director and several part-time assistants from the teaching and sodality staff who do regular spiritual counseling and organize and promote an extensive program of religious exercises for the University students. Besides these professedly spiritual and religious facilities we have the Psychological Services Center which is professionally staffed and equipped to do testing and counseling in all areas: spiritual, vocational, educational and psychological. Students come to the Center either on their own initiative or on referral by deans, spiritual counselors, faculty members, academic advisers, parents, or even by a fellow student or friend.

During our eight years of operation at the Center we, that is, the three other psychologists (Laymen) and I, have slowly developed the practice of using a non-authoritative and permissive relationship with our students until we feel that they have come to understand themselves and have begun at least to be self-directive. Then we will give them any tests that they may request and any information that they may need, or refer them to psychiatrists and psychological clinics for further diagnosis and further therapy.

We said "further" therapy designedly because we have found that non-authoritative and permissive counseling does produce therapeutic effects by enabling the student to reorganize his emotional reactions. Then he can, as Father Curran puts it, not only choose better ways to reach his reasonable goals, but also will have sufficient confidence, courage and moderation to act on these choices.

Let us briefly discuss referrals. If you find from your permissive and non-authoritative counseling that the student's religious or moral maladjustments are so deep-seated that counseling will not solve them, then knowledge of reliable and capable psychiatrists and diocesan and community psychological clinics is required. If you have this information gathered and classified in your office, you will be able to make more effective referrals. Because psychological and medical services are of their very nature expensive, information regarding fees and knowledge of services that scale their fees in proportion to the client's ability to pay is very important. But, even with the best efforts on your part, you will still have students who will refuse to take advantage of psychological or psychiatric services even though they need them desperately.

We have said that, after the student has come to understand and accept the emotional roots of his religious and moral problems through non-authoritative and permissive counseling, then we may become advisers as well as counselors and give him any particular information or refer him to any therapeutic services his condition may require. [5]

Testing and the Religious Counselor

Now let us consider briefly psychological testing as an aid in religious and moral counseling. What should be our attitude toward tests and how should we administer and interpret them? We believe that tests can be of great help in many cases but that they are not always necessary. We never impose tests upon students except when the student has been referred by a dean, teacher or employer with an explicit request for psychological testing. In a case of this kind, and especially when the student is opposed to taking tests and may be antagonistic and resentful, we try by non-authoritative and permissive counseling to get him to accept his situation and to accept us as means of better self-understanding and self-direction.

Before we give a test we should carefully explain to the student in words that he can understand what the test is supposed to do and how accurate it is in doing it. Then in the interpretation of the results of the test we must be just as careful to tell the student once more what the test was supposed to do and about how accurate his score and ratings are.

Personality tests are, of course, potentially the most useful in counseling students with religious and emotional problems. We say "potentially the most useful," because actually the results of personality tests have to be used with the greatest discernment and discretion. Of all our tests personality tests suffer the most in reliability and validity. For this reason we must study the results of the test very thoroughly before we discuss it with the student. We should make an item analysis of the test, that is, go through the test to find the items that gave the student an unfavorable score. Then we should discuss these items with the student and encourage him to give his reaction to the unfavorable scores and to the items that resulted in unfavorable scores.

Religious counselors should not use certain individual personality tests, like the Rorschach, or even group tests like the Minnesota Multiphasic or Bernreuter Personality Inventory, unless they are well trained in their administration and interpretation. The poor use of personality tests can do serious harm and increase and intensify personality difficulties rather than solve them.

The Mooney Problem Check List

There are, however, personality (or adjustment) inventories that can be used effectively even by counselors without special training in personality testing and interpretation. The Mooney Problem Check List [6] in an instrument of this kind. In reality it is not a test but a check-list method of observing personal problems, a kind of controlled interview. This inventory has a section of religious and moral problems which is especially helpful, but the religious counselor will learn to use the other sections of home, health, personal, social problems, and so forth, as leads to the more deeply rooted causes of the counselee's religious and moral problems. Some of the religious and moral problems which our religious counselors at the University of Detroit deal with are peculiar to Catholic students. A special one-page list of the problems that have been dealt with locally has been compiled. The list is used either as a supplement to the Mooney Problem Check List or in place of it according to the judgment of the religious counselor.

Of course, there is always the danger that the counselee will not be serious and honest in taking the inventory. We have found that the following procedures prevent this. First of all, the counselee is told that the counselor will go through the inventory with him in his conference. Furthermore he is assured that his answers will be kept in the strictest confidence and that no one else will have access to the results of the test without his written permission. For this reason it is best if the counselee is given the inventory by himself. If it is given in a group, then the counselor, and not a teacher or any administrative officer, should give it and assure the group that the inventory will be used by the counselor only in a later conference with the counselee.

We have found that a problem inventory like the Mooney Problem Check List may do several things for the counselee. It often reminds him of problems that he might otherwise not recall during the actual counseling session. Secondly, it often is easier to talk about certain of his problems once he has checked them on the printed page. Finally, the opportunity that he is given in the inventory to write a brief summary of his chief problems affords him emotional release for the interview. Of course, counselees will vary in their response to this opportunity. Some will write nothing at all, many will write a short paragraph, a few will attach a page or two. In any case, the Mooney Problem Check List can be a great help in preparing the counselee for counseling and, properly handled, can become an integral part of a permissive counseling relationship.

Summary, Conclusion

We shall now summarize and conclude our discussion. We have distinguished between religious advising and religious counseling. They are both important and helpful activities, but they are quite different. Religious advising is authoritative and directive. It often becomes a form of teaching. The adviser tells his advisee what he should know and what he should do. Because of his greater knowledge and experience he gives his advisee the knowledge and direction that the latter needs. Religious counseling on the other hand is non-authoritative, permissive and non-directive. Counsel is a habit that must be acquired by the counselee's own acts. The counselor cannot give it to him. The counselor can only provide the non-authoritative and permissive atmosphere in which the counselee can survey the past and present factors which enter into his personal confusions and conflicts. He then is better able to reorganize his emotional reactions so that he can, not only choose better ways to reach his reasonable goals, but will also have sufficient confidence, courage and moderation to act on these choices. The counselee counsels himself helped by the sensitive understanding and permissive atmosphere supplied by the counselor. By repeated acts of thus counseling himself, the counselee acquires or forms the habit of counsel, a possession of priceless worth in these days of perplexities and confusions.

REFERENCES

1. Rogers, C.R. *Counseling and Psycotherapy.* Boston: Houghton Mifflin, 1942.
   Rogers, C.R. *Client Centered Therapy.* Boston: Houghton Mifflin, 1951.
   Rogers, C.R. *On Becoming a Person.* Boston: Houghton Mifflin, 1961.
2. Curran, Rev. C.A. *Counseling in Catholic Life and Education.* New York: Macmillan, 1952, p. 452.
3. Curran, Rev. C.A. *Personality Factors in Counseling.* New York: Grune and Stratton, 1945, p. 260.
4. For some practical problems, cf. Hagmaier, G. and Gleason, R. *Counselling the Catholic.* New York: Sheed and Ward, 1959.
5. For a discussion of different approaches of the pastor to his counselees, cf. Godin, A. *The Pastor as Counselor.* New York: Holt, Rinehart and Winston, 1965.
6. There are four forms of the Mooney Problem Check List: J, for junior high school pupils; H, for high school students; C, for college students; and A, for adults. The lists are published by the psychological Corporation, 304 East 45 Street, New York, New York 10017.

EVALUATION AND GRASS ROOTS RESEARCH

WILLIAM C. COTTLE
*Director of the Counselor Education and Counseling
Psychology Programs, and Professor of Education,
Boston College*

*Dr. Cottle shows that for an evaluation of the guidance program
it is necessary to begin with a criterion ("What do I want these boys
and girls to be able to do?"). He indicates the importance of evaluative reports to administrators, parents, teachers, and students.*

*Related to evaluation is the work of grass roots research, and
Dr. Cottle maintains that this should flow from the counselor's immediate work. He illustrates the process of grass roots research with
his own studies which developed out of his counseling experiences with two widely used testing instruments. Many administrators
and counselors will read with interest and anticipate final publication of Dr. Cottle's Dropout Inventory.*

To begin this topic it is probably better to raise questions
than to attempt to provide answers. The first question is, "Evaluate what?"

It seems we could say first of all we want to evaluate what
the guidance worker is trying to do. Whatever you want included
in your guidance program should be included also in the process
of evaluation. But it has to relate to *your* program of guidance
services. You can not pick up some canned evaluation program
and expect to come out of it with any kind of effective evaluation of your own particular program.

You have to start out by saying, "What is it I am trying to
accomplish in this job?" And list these things. Then say to
yourself, "How do I hope to do this?" The more complex, the
more involved you try to make your program, the more difficult
it is to find an evaluative process and to identify statistics which
will show what you are doing. And in the final analysis you must

147

be able to justify any program in order to get money to continue it, whether it is for your own salary or to carry on activities helpful to students.

After you have figured out what you are trying to do and how you are going to do it, then you begin to wonder, "What do I hope will happen here? What do I want to show is happening? How do I go about it?" Then this becomes an individual question and answer period for yourself. Nobody can help you with it. You may go to some statistician and say, "Here is what I am trying to do. Here is what I am trying to demonstrate. Will these statistics accomplish it?" It is better to go with some ideas, than to go and say to this person, "This is what I hope to do. How can I do it?" If you go without any proposal, he may get you so involved that before you are through you quit and just do not evaluate at all. Statisticians can get pretty involved in any statistical process, so you should go to them and say, "Here are the things I want to do, and here are the ways I think I can do them. Do they make sense?" Then you are in a much better position because you are telling them that you have been doing some thinking about this, you have some ideas, and they can fill in the blank spots or support the weak spots or whatever is necessary in order to help you do the job of evaluation.

SEEKING A CRITERION

One of the problems you will encounter is what is called in tests and measurements, the "problems of an adequate criterion." This means really, "How do I show that I have been doing this." There was a meeting on our campus several months ago at which a school superintendent asked "What do you do about parental demands? All we are able to do in our guidance program is help parents get their children into college." Someone needs to say to a person like this, "If I had a guidance program and seniors in my school did not know how to fill out application forms and write for college catalogues, and figure out where they wanted to go to school, I would be pretty ashamed of the program."

This is one of the criteria. Can the students function effectively after they have been through this process that we call guidance services? And it seems that this may be the primary criterion, so one of the questions you have to ask yourself when you are establishing these criteria is, "What do I want these boys and girls to be able to do?" It is as simple as that. If you can list these things in order, then, you can set up means of testing to see whether the boys and girls can do them or not. This is the first question you need to ask, the criterion of performance.

A question related to the criterion of performance centers around the difficulties inherent in identifying characteristics contributing to successful performance. Different individuals use different skills to achieve the same task. For example, one student may use a high level of verbal-linguistic skills to compensate for weakness in quantitative skills and still be a graduate of an engineering school where most graduates are highly proficient in quantitative skills. There are also many different kinds of engineers. It is difficult to say, "All engineers have to perform these activities in order to function effectively as engineers." It is much simpler to go the other way around and say, "What are common requirements that these engineers must surmount?"

Perhaps a more meaningful illustration would be the amount of education necessary to qualify for state certification as a counselor. If a person does not meet this requirement, obviously he is not going to be a counselor. In most states he must have a prescribed number of graduate semester hours in given course areas. This is one criterion that can be established. If the person is not able to complete the necessary number of courses to function as a certified counselor, then this is one way of deciding that this person will not become a counselor.

Another criterion in counseling which sometimes occurs at the end of academic work is exemplified by the individual who gets all through courses for a Masters degree, and then goes into practicum and demonstrates that he cannot handle people in a one-to-one situation. This is unfortunate, but if it is really true and not just a case of stage fright, this is another negative indicator. We may not be able to pick out the common characteristics of people who will be the good counselors, but we can find the people in a practicum setting who will not be able to function adequately as counselors. The same sort of things happen in terms of other criteria. If positive criteria cannot be identified at least we can set up negative criteria, and by process of elimination be able to identify the people who are unable to qualify. Then it will be possible to work out some system of helping them learn ways of mastering these hurdles or choosing other objectives. Perhaps they can perform other guidance activities.

Getting back to the evaluation process, it is necessary to identify the places where criterion information is available. In setting up criteria to evaluate a guidance program it is essential to ask, "What are the goals of these students? What do they want to accomplish, either in current education, further education, or on the job." And therefore, "What criteria can I select to evaluate this process? How many of these people went on to further education, completed it successfully, and how many did not? How many people went into jobs and functioned successfully on the jobs, and how many did not? And what part did the program of guidance services play in this?"

This is the difficult question. If they all went through the program of guidance services, how do you demonstrate that those who failed did so because they did not get as much out of the program of guidance services, and not because of some basic weakness in the educational program.

WHO NEEDS EVALUATIVE DATA?

Another question that the counselor has to ask himself here is, "What persons am I trying to satisfy? Are they administrators?" It is essential to furnish administrators information in terms of facts and figures that show that the guidance program is worth spending money to maintain. They in turn will have to go to a superior, or to a parent group, or to some other group and be able to demonstrate the value of spending money on the program of guidance services. Unless it is possible to furnish these data, the guidance program is going to be in trouble financially.

Is it teachers the counselor is trying to satisfy? Perhaps this can be done by showing them how the program of guidance services can make their job easier and by showing them how their activities and efforts can make the guidance program more effective. The counselor should collect this evaluation material in a way that will show this. How this is done depends on each individual situation, but the counselor has to know the teachers well enough to be able to go to them and say, "Is this program of guidance services of any value to you?" If the answer is generally, "No," then either the counselor does not have an effective program or it is not being communicated well to the teachers. The counselor can say, "Here are the ways in which I need your help." It seems easier to get somebody to give help than to go to him and say, "I would like to give you help."

Is it the parents who must have information about the value of the program? In some schools the parents get the least consideration of any one. Perhaps you will say, "In terms of my experience with them, they deserve it." But in many school settings we have a tendency to forget parents and the fact that because they have problems, maybe the students with whom we work, have more problems. If we were able to help the parents in some way we might thus reduce the number of problems the students encounter. Even the counselor, who is also a parent, needs help. Such a counselor can usually work effectively with other people's children to help them to accomplish the things they want to achieve, but he, as other parents, gets emotionally involved where his own children are concerned. Parents need help in organizing their feelings so that they too can work well with their children. This ultimately reduces the work the counselor needs to include in the guidance program and therefore the amount that must be evaluated.

Maybe we should have considered the next group first instead of last—the clients, the boys and girls with whom the counselor works. Certainly if any group needs to be happy and satisfied with the program of guidance services, they do. The counselor cannot afford to have them get the feeling that this is a private snake pit where the counselor probes to uncover all the personal problems and conflicts they have. They need to have the feeling that here is a person who is sympathetic, but not in an emotional, "bleeding-heart" way. Here is a person who can understand the things that they are trying to say, a person who knows places they can go to get information, but not necessarily a person who knows all the information. No counselor could hope to acquire in one life time all the information a series of students come in and request in the space of a year. But the counselor ought to know where this information *can* be secured. These clients also need to feel that here is a person who can listen. One of the important points to be considered by beginning counselors is the fact that they were given two ears but only one tongue. These remarks conclude the questions raised concerning evaluation.

GRASS ROOTS RESEARCH

Another topic which does not create the same sort of pressure that evaluating a guidance program does is the problem of grass roots research. It evolves logically out of the program of evaluation. When we consider and discuss research, we have a tendency to get "graduate studentitis." This is the tendency to make any problem as complex as possible because it makes you feel more competent when, and if, you solve it. It is like driving a large expensive car instead of a compact; it will not get you there much quicker, but you may feel better going, wherever you think you are going.

Research Grows From Daily Work

The way in which to develop ideas for grass roots research, or any research, is in terms of the immediate work you are trying to do. Try to keep your ears and eyes open and your mouth closed, as much as possible. If you are able to do this in the process of counseling some questions will always arise. You suspect as you talk to one boy and another boy and another boy, that you see a pattern of behavior developing with common elements from boy to boy. You say to yourself, "Is this true or is it my imagination?" And here is your research problem. It does not have to be very involved. One of the things that has helped me to accomplish research has been the fact that I have had so many graduate students come in and say, "I have to write a thesis," or "I've got to write a research paper at the end of my Master's program. What shall I do?" Somehow in 30 hours of graduate work they never develop this very simple concept, that *research results from looking for answers to questions you have about your daily work.* This does not mean that it is necessary to get involved in elaborate statistics. It is necessary to use statistics to answer any question, because it is necessary to quantify the material. Use the statistics that are necessary to do the job, and if simple percentages will work, why be fancy? Tests of significance can be done with percentages as well as with means. The statistics that are used need to be practical. They need to be something that will demonstrate that there are or are not differences between the groups being compared. They need to provide the answers with a minimum amount of work. In the process of doing this it is important to seek various sorts of answers. Answers that give results of current efforts and answers that show the direction of future activity.

To illustrate this point, in the process of my own activities in counseling I have gotten interested recently in two simple but important problems. The first is the effect that an individual's response set defined as his "general tendency to respond," has upon test results and upon his behavior in general. The other is seeking a way to identify school dropouts before they leave school so a counselor can help them make as effective a placement as possible.

Response Set Research

Let us look for a moment at the problem of client response set and how this can make the counselor's job of interpreting test scores more meaningful. We have been exploring at Boston College some of the more commonly used interest and personality inventories and some of the problems in connection with them. There are some people who can pick up the profile of a Kuder Preference Record-Vocational and begin to read off extensive client information. They have never seen the profile on the inventory before, they have never read the manual, but this is the Kuder and it is easy to use. There are other people who try to do the same thing with the profile of the Minnesota Multiphasic Personality Inventory (MMPI) and the Strong Vocational Interest Blank (SVIB). Neither one of these inventories is very simple to use once you begin to work with them and get to know the complex data they are indicating.

The MMPI

One of the first things that interested me in response set research was some work with the Minnesota Multiphasic Personality Inventory (MMPI) at the University of Kansas a number of years ago. [1] We were interested in what would happen if a client answered the MMPI in some random fashion, instead of doing it as most people would by answering *true, false,* or *cannot say* to each item. We decided we would take twenty-five answer sheets and use a pair of dice to determine the answers to each item. We took another twenty-five answer sheets and used a table of random numbers to answer each of the 566 items on the booklet form of the MMPI. When compared to college students these random profiles are considerably different. The mean profiles of college students tend to be approximately one-half standard deviation above the mean of the standardization group for the MMPI. The mean of the random profiles is at a T score equivalent to about half the possible raw score for each scale, a point considerably above the mean for the college population on each scale.

What this is saying is that the integrating force of an individual's personality is needed to produce the checks and balances that produce a profile within the normal range. There is another way to check this. We took two answer sheets and on one, we marked all the items *true.* This produces a profile which is obviously an invalid profile, with the scales of the psychotic triad the extremely elevated ones. When the inventory is marked all *false* there is a pronounced elevation on the scales of the neurotic triad and a tendency toward an extreme neurotic profile. But these profiles are also telling something else: that when this rise appears in the neurotic triad on an individual profile it indicates that the client has answered more items false than true. Conversely, when the high scores are on the psychotic scales on an individual's profile he has answered more items true than false. This tendency to respond in a given direction, true *or* false, is in part responsible for the profile that the individual achieves on this particular instrument.

Notice the two things that this research is emphasizing. One, a profile within the normal range is not produced by random methods. It has to be something describing behavior of a given individual, which takes into account checks and balances producing this normal profile. And two, if an individual has a tendency to respond in a given direction, either more true than false, or more false than true, it will distort the profile toward the psychotic or toward the neurotic scales of the inventory, respectively. This confuses two different kinds of information: those responses reflecting specific personality traits and those which reflect a more general response set tendency. So one of the first things a counselor should seek when he looks at the MMPI profile is a count of the number of true responses and of the number of false responses, so that he can see what is happening in terms of response set.

Response Sets on the Strong

A couple of years ago I also became interested in the effect of response set on scores of the Strong Vocational Interest Blank (SVIB). So last year I took answer sheets for the Women's Strong, (SVIB-W) and I marked one all *like,* another one all *indifferent,* and a third one all *dislike.* These profiles indicate that if a client marks all SVIB-W items *like,* she gets a low score on woman librarian and a very feminine score on the masculinity-femininity scale. She gets high scores on woman social worker, woman lawyer, and the so-called "non-career" group of housewife, elementary teacher, stenographer-secretary, business education teacher, and office worker. At the same time four of these non-career patterns appear as high interest patterns, if she marks all *indifferent.* Yet for years we have been saying, "Why is it that when you give women the Strong Vocation Interest Blank they get high scores on these particular scales?" In the past these scales have been called non-career occupations because they are the occupations that most women enter temporarily until they marry and raise a family. It was assumed that most women score high because there is a common pattern for women. Yet it is obvious now that any combination which produces a predominance of *like* and *indifferent* responses is going to result in this pattern and it is not an occupational pattern at all. It is a function of the individual's response set and the format of the instrument.

Let us look at some of the other response set scores. With a preponderance of like responses a female client would also get high scores on home economics teacher, nurse and on physical therapist.

With a preponderance of *indifferent* responses she would get a low score on author. She would get a score on the masculine side of the MF scale and, as indicated above, high scores on the four non-career occupations. She would also get high scores for physical education teacher—college, occupational therapist, math science teacher, laboratory technician, physical therapist and woman engineer.

When the blank is marked preponderantly *dislike,* she gets low scores on social worker, social science teacher, YWCA secretary, home economics teacher physical education teacher—college, occupational therapist, nurse, musician-teacher, physical therapist and woman engineer. And she gets high scores on artist, author, librarian, and woman physician. With a preponderance of *dislike* responses the masculinity-feminity score again is in the masculine direction. This may mean that any combination of *dislike* and *indifferent* scores can produce a masculine interest on the SVIB-W and it is not necessarily produced because this person really has a masculine interest pattern when compared to most other women. It may again be a function of the response set of the individual acting upon the test.

Meaning of Response Sets

Now what does this mean? Do you have to distrust the Strong Vocational Interest Blank at this point? The answer is not clear. What it seems to be saying is that wherever it is possible to get high scores through all *like,* all *dislike,* or all *indifferent* responses, the counselor should look very carefully at the number of like, indifferent, and dislike responses this individual has made to this blank before scores can be discussed as being a real occupational interest pattern. That is the first conclusion. The second conclusion that the counselor makes is, "If the client makes this kind of response, it may be a part the pattern of people in that occupation to have this kind of response set. So it may be just as useful to me as if I got what I could truly label an occupational interest pattern."

A Dropout Inventory

Earlier, mention was made of the work we have been doing in attempting to develop a scale which will identify dropouts before they leave school, so that a counselor could work with them and see what is necessary to help them make the most effective placement. Sometimes helping them stay in school is not the most effective answer to their problems or to their placement. They may have had just as much school as they can use and they might better be out working somewhere, or in some specialized training that the school cannot offer.

A number of years ago a student of mine wanted to do a study in Topeka High School as an attempt to predict dropouts. So he took a number of elements like grade point average, the number of days absent, and other material that he could pick from the school records, such as intelligence test scores or achievement test scores. He tried to make a predictor out of these, teacher ratings and peer group ratings. None of them was particularly effective. There was a statistically significant difference when he used any one of these three predictors, but not a practical difference so that he could look at them without the statistics and say this pupil is apt to be a dropout.

In the process of this research it struck me that everybody studies dropouts after they have left school, but nobody does much about trying to identify them while they are in school, either to help them stay, or to help them find a better job, or to help them find other kinds of education or some more effective placement if they leave school. The literature on dropouts showed about fifteen characteristics that seemed to describe most dropouts, such things as that they were overage in grade, or that they have more frequent absences, or that many of them come from homes of low socio-economic status. From these fifteen characteristics I made up a series of 150 items, about ten for each one.

Then we gave it to eighth and ninth graders in the Topeka school system and waited two years to see who dropped out. We took the number of dropouts and from the rest who stayed in school we drew an equal number at random. (If you are going to do research of any kind, it is much simpler to use groups of equal number because there are a lot of short cut statistical methods for equal numbers.)

We identified the items out of this 150 which would describe differences between these two groups—the ones who stayed in school and the ones who dropped out. Then we made up a scale keyed in the direction of dropout responses. We gave this to another group of pupils in the Kansas City area and found that the same items would identify pupils who would drop out of school in the Kansas City area. Different scales emerged, however, for boys and for girls, with some of the items common to boys and to girls, but many of them different. Houghton Mifflin Company is sharing further research on the School Interest Inventory with me and, if it proves effective, they will publish it.

We are starting now to get a national sample. As soon as we find out whether the inventory works on a national sample we will be able to offer the inventory to people in counseling positions in schools who want to identify pupils who are apt to drop out. Then the counselors can work with them to see if they can help them to make a more effective placement.

Notice that this last research has had limited publication. Bits and pieces of it have been published in the literature as preliminary reports of research in progress, but nothing is published completely or offered for sale, because we do not have enough research information yet to be able to say, "This will work in your school."

Here then, are two areas that could be classified as "grass roots research." For the first area questions that a counselor could ask himself are, "What do the responses really mean on the Strong Vocational Interest Blank, or the Multiphasic, or any of the other tests I use? What do I really know about them?" And for the other one, "What can I do about school dropouts?"

We have tried to consider two related topics in this approach: How the daily questions that a guidance worker asks as an outgrowth of work experiences can become the focus of meaningful evaluation, and how they develop into research projects in order to accomplish this purpose.

REFERENCE

1. Cottle, W. C. and Powell, J. O., Random Answers to the MMPI. *Educational and Psychological Measurement*, 11, 1951, 224-227.

REFERENCES FOR FURTHER READING

Berdie, R. F., et al. *Testing in Guidance and Counseling.* New York: McGraw Hill, Ch. 14, 1963.

Corey, S. M. *Action Research to Improve School Practices.* New York: Bureau of Publications, Teachers College, Columbia U., 1953.

Cottle, W. C. and Downie, N. M. *Procedures and Preparation for Counseling.* New York: Prentice-Hall, Ch. 12, 1960.

Goldman, L. *Using Tests in Counseling.* New York: Appleton-Century-Crofts, Inc., 1961.

A GUIDANCE PROGRAM AND
AN EVALUATION

by

THOMAS C. HENNESSY, S.J.

Assistant Professor

The School of Education, Fordham University

Often prospective counselors wish to read an outline of the activities of an actually functioning guidance program. The first part of the following paper offers such a description. After a brief statement about the type of school being described—a Catholic school—and its guidance staff, seven of the usual elements of the guidance program are described. Certain other parts of the usual program are not included because of lack of space, such as testing, information services and the student follow-up.

In Part II of the paper each of the seven services named above is evaluated, or else for an obvious reason, an evaluation is regarded as unnecessary. The training of the guidance staff is regarded as inferior. No rating is offered with regard to the Admission of Students and the Health Service. The school's Orientation and Adjustment of New Students is rated as good. The Student Records system is regarded as average. The counseling services—often called the heart of guidance—is judged to be superior. The area of Discipline is viewed as average. The Placement of students after high school is concluded to be superior.

In the course of the evaluation certain recommendations are made. Among them are: counselors in all schools should receive professional training for their work; the administration take an active role in fostering group guidance; a separate records department with easy access for faculty members be provided in each school; whenever possible the religious counselor be the general guidance counselor; schools should integrate a religious program in their guidance activities; counselors should help in school discipline as consultants on behavior and as rehabilitation agents.

PART I

The School

The school is a private secondary school of excellent reputation in a large city. It is situated near a college campus in an area which is a mixture of business and lower middle class homes. Transportation facilities of all types are at hand, and as a result students come from many different neighborhoods to attend the school. It has been established for over a century and is filled with many traditions. In this paper names are omitted, and some details changed, but the school and the program really exists.

The school building itself is quite plain and can contain between 800 and 900 students. The exact number depends upon the success of the students in "measuring up" to the demands of their courses, and upon the current financial prosperity. Tuition of $450.00 per annum is charged.

There are three main courses, with variations, which students must enter upon after their first year. In first year all students are engaged in the same courses. After that they must be enrolled in the honors Greek, the honors science, or the general course. However, each student must complete three years of Latin, four years of English, three years of mathematics, two years of a modern language (German, French or Russian). Competition to enter the school is quite keen, and scholarship rewards at the end of the course are quite numerous.

Extracurricular opportunities at the school are varied and well attended. Varsity sports include football, basketball, swimming, track, and handball, and there is also a vigorous program of intramural sports. Furthermore dramatics, debating, writing in the school newspaper, magazine and yearbook, and numerous other activities keep busy the after-school hours of many a student and many a moderator.

The school is Catholic and is directed by a religious order. Religious instruction and brief group prayer are integral elements of the daily school activity. Special religious exercises are held weekly (Mass), monthly (Benediction and sermon) and annually (the retreat, held either at school or at special retreat houses).

The Guidance Personnel

The staff of the school is composed about equally of priests, seminarians who have usually completed seven years of ecclesiastical and college study, and lay teachers, many of whom have taught in the school long enough to consider it their life's work. All of the school officials and student counselors are priests.

Each of the school officials contributes towards the guidance program. The principal has ultimate responsibility both for the management of the program and for the assignment and evaluation of personnel. Students and parents will often come to him for advice particularly on educational, and personal difficulties. Much of his time is used for this during school hours and indeed after school hours and on holidays. The prefect of discipline, sometimes called the assistant principal, understands that breaking of school regulations may well be caused by more serious personal or religious difficulties. Students learn that his knowledge of boys is not just connected with external habits, but with their psychology and problems as well. The prefect of athletics, too, finds that his close relationship with the students in their athletic successes and failures provides him with much opportunity to guide them in situations which are kindred to what will come their way in later life. All other moderators of extracurricular activities are urged to view their work as an opportunity to guide in a religious and educational way those who come in closest contact with them.

Classroom teachers are regarded by the administration as counselors to the students whom they teach. However, the administration has never required that group guidance or interviewing be done by the classroom teachers. No special time is set aside for these activities. Some of the teachers react to this permissive atmosphere by a minimum amount of concern and guidance for their students, while the majority spend a great deal of time assisting their charges. The school's high academic standards and general good "school spirit" may be a reflection of the dedication of the latter group of teachers.

While so many members of the staff contribute towards effective guidance, to the student counselors is entrusted much of the official responsibiity in this field. There is a full-time student counselor and full-time assistant student counselor. The office of the student counselor adjoins the principal's office where all school records are filed. The office of the assistant student counselor is on the other side of the hall, opposite the student counselor's office.

The student counselors make themselves available to all students before school, during recess and after school. During class time the student counselors interview the students, conduct tests or give group guidance talks.

In the fall term senior students have lengthy interviews with the student counselor to review their vocational and educational plans and to provide opportunity to discuss personal or family problems. In the spring term he interviews the third year students to discuss the same matters. The assistant student counselor interviews all first year and second year students. All students know that they may come for an interview after class whenever they wish, to either student counselor. They also know that the student counselors have nothing at all to do with discipline in the school. It is as though "never the twain shall meet."

The qualifications of the staff for counseling and guidance are based primarily upon their religious training. All the priests have studied the many shades and shadows of human behavior in their courses in moral theology. A major element in the motivation of all members of religious orders pertains to the sacredness and respect for each human person. Hence there is a deep concern for each person's way of thinking and his actions. Clearly these attitudes which are shared by the religious and lay members of the faculty set the foundation for a good guidance program.

There has been little academic, specialized training of the faculty or of the counselors for their work. However, both counselors attended two summer institutes on the counseling process and on the organization and development of the guidance program. They continue to do some reading along lines suggested in the summer institutes. For additional stimulation the counselors attend the semiannual all-day workshops conducted by their local diocesan guidance council.

The Guidance Program

Following the lead of Andrew and Willey [1], the following headings will be used to report the high school's gudiance services:

1. Admission of students.
2. Orientation, adjustment of new students.
3. Students records, academic and non-academic.
4. Counseling:
   a. Educational.
   b. Vocational.
   c. Personal (moral, social).
5. Health service.
6. Discipline.
7. Placement service.

1. **Admission of students** is by competitive examination only through the Cooperative Entrance Examination for the 225 seats available for the entering class. Usually about 1200 students apply for admission. The pupils at the top of the competitive examination are invited to register. This competitive entrance examination is open to any boy who has completed the eighth grade in the public or parochial schools. The examination in English and Arithmetic is devised and scored by the Harcourt, Brace and World Book Company.

This aspect of guidance is administered by the principal.

2. **Orientation and adjustment of new students.** Parents or guardians of incoming freshmen are given a copy of the Bulletin of Information to acquaint them with the school's history, philosophy and system of education, school regulations and courses. They also receive a letter just before entrance day informing them of the order to be followed for the first week of school.

Incoming freshmen are in school the week preceding the return of the upper classmen. They have group guidance sessions which pertain to their obligations to God, country, and fellowman; and they are offered motives for study and application during their high school career. They learn the customs of the school with regard to the social, academic and disciplinary activity.

In the course of the first few weeks moderators of the different activities extend an invitation to the new students to join their organizations.

About a month after the new students come to the school, the first parents' meeting, for parents of freshmen, takes place. Parents have the opportunity to meet their sons' teachers and officials of the school.

3. **Student records, academic and non-academic.** Records in the principal's office contain complete data concerning each student, his attendance, his I.Q., parish, picture, former school, name and address of parents and their business, telephone number, academic grades and honors and other pertinent matters. These records may be seen by teachers upon request. They are cumulative for the student's stay in school.

Besides, there is a separate folder for each student in which more personal matters are kept, for example, correspondence between school authorities and parents, as well as health records. This folder is private.

The complete record of a student's discipline and attendance is kept in the prefect of discipline's office. In addition, the prefect of discipline has a book in which is kept the pertinent factual data about the student, address, telephone, previous school, etc.

The student counselor also has a folder for each student, and keeps therein:

> the questionnaire, autobiographical in nature, which is filled in during the student's first few days in school; the follow-up on this questionnaire, which is given in third year;
>
> ability tests;
>
> preference tests (the Kuder Preference Record, Vocational, and in some cases, the Strong Vocational Interest Blank for Men);
>
> personality rating card made out by teachers;
>
> a picture of the student;
>
> a brief record of interviews, covering the general subjects treated if they are educational or vocational in nature;

Bell Adjustment Inventory Record.

These records are of great use to the student counselors during their interviews. It is understood that most of the student counselors' files are confidential, though the results of the standardized tests are freely given to teachers upon request. The counselor's records are kept intact until five years after the student leaves the school; they are then destroyed.

4. Counseling

a. **Educational.** Because of the typical rapport between teachers and students, teachers consider it their duty to guide the student informally. The personal interest of the teachers in each student is a reality not appearing upon the records and yet is one of the best elements of the school. The class teacher knows the students by their first names and because of his interest in the young and his love of them is in a position to advise the principal and the parents when some problems arise in reference to the students.

The choice of the course that the student will take has to be made towards the end of first year. The student makes a choice after receiving advice from his teachers, who weigh his talent, his personality and goal in life. Students are urged not to undertake the added burden of the honors course unless it is deemed likely that they can see their way to success in it.

Deficiencies are made known to parents through report cards six times a year. Failures are reported to parents through a special card sent to them in the mail. Teachers give to the principal a written report on the reason for a student s failure at the conclusion of each marking period. Furthermore, the principal has a conference with each class teacher about the marks of each student at the close of each marking period. Parents are encouraged to consult with the principal and the student's teachers, particularly when he has failed a subject. Thus parents are warned of a student's possible or probable failure for the term.

The student's fourth year interview is largely concerned with his vocational and educational planning. If he plans to continue his education he and the student counselor work out together the schools and the course that seems best for him, in view of his high school record and talents, as revealed by the tests and other data at the disposal of the student counselor.

College representatives are invited to see students after school time.

b. **Vocational.** In the questionnaire which they fill out in first year, the students are asked to write down their vocational plans. They are also asked to state their vocational decisions in the follow-up third year questionnaire. And during their third and fourth year interviews, they go over this matter with the student counselor.

To help them to a decision with regard to vocation, the Kuder Preference Record, which offers scores in ten different areas, is administered to students in their third year. Besides, the Merit Scholarship Test, Primary Mental Abilities, the SCAT (School and College Ability Test) and the NEDT (National Educational Development Tests) provide data to indicate the areas of their best aptitudes. Most of these tests are interpreted for them in the third year interview and they are asked to think over their vocation with the knowledge of their strongest area of preference and aptitudes in mind.

The students are urged to use extensively the vocational literature and file which is readily available in the school library.

Students who seem to be still indefinite with regard to vocation in their fourth year complete the Strong Vocational Interest Blank for Men.

When the senior reviews his vocational plans with the student counselor, a regular part of the interview calls his reading the pertinent article in the latest *Occupational Outlook Handbook* published by the U.S. Department of Labor, or the leaflets provided by New York Life Insurance Co., or similar publications.

Group guidance talks are given to each class by the student counselor before students of a given class have their regular interviews. For instance, in third year, talks are given about how to choose a college, the general principles connected with choosing a college major, how to apply to a college, how to read a college catalogue, scholarship opportunities and other pertinent topics.

c. **Personal** (Health, civic, moral, social). This is accomplished in three ways, through interviews, group guidance and the religious program.

(1) *Interviews.* As in the case of educational and vocational guidance, the student knows that he can consult often with his

class teachers, the moderators of the different activities, and the two student counselors. Students do use this service. One of the students while urging elementary school children to attend the high school said, "You can talk to the teachers about *anything*."

(2) *Group Guidance*. As indicated earlier, teachers are encouraged to utilize opportunities for group guidance, but are not required to do so. A questionnaire distributed by the guidance department to the faculty indicated that group guidance was professedly engaged in by one tenth of the faculty. They showed a preference for the *Insight* series. [2] The fact that so small a percentage of the faculty participate in group guidance activities reflects the permissive attitude of the administration. Perhaps this area requires additional investigation.

(3) *The Religious Program*. While the religious instruction department is separate from the guidance department, the school's philosophy requires an integration of guidance and religious practices. Within this general religious frame of reference, the freedom of the individual is completely respected. As a member of the school, he is expected to attend with his peers the instruction and religious exercises which are provided. Each school day begins with a minute or two of vocal prayer. There is a full period of religious instruction each school day; the instruction is in accordance with the syllabus which includes the areas of the dogmatic and moral teaching of the Catholic Church. Through this instruction a unified philosophy towards life is taught. Values that follow in the wake of this philosophy are usually absorbed. Guidance is deeply concerned with students' philosophy and values and often informal group guidance sessions develop in the religious instruction class.

Another element of the religious program is the use of the sacrament of penance. One day a week students are urged to make use of this spiritual opportunity. It enables the student not only to obtain the forgiveness of his sins but also to discuss with the priest any topic which he may wish to bring up. Furthermore, there is ample opportunity to "go to confession" before or after school. Since the student may introduce the most troublesome and personal topics in the confessional, it is easy to see that the guidance ideals of self-understanding and decision-making are facilitated through this means.

Though there are other religious elements in the school which are associated with guidance, only one final aspect will be mentioned. It is the retreat program. Students in the first and second year make the retreat at school, usually in the early part of the academic year. Those in third and fourth year make a "closed" retreat, which requires that they spend three days away from home in a large residence which has ideal conditions for prayer and meditation. During the retreats, especially the "closed" ones, students have an excellent atmosphere for considering themselves and their problems. Group instruction and prayer is the order of the day. They are urged to discuss their problems with a counselor. That the retreats have helped to achieve the goal of increasing personal understanding and peace has been spontaneously attested to by many students. Many of them consider these days the best days of their life. Problems are examined, and sometimes solved. Decisions are made. Thus the goals of guidance are achieved through the retreat program.

The work of sex education is achieved through the combination of religious instruction, confession, retreats and the personal interview. Particularly during the closed retreat, the youths are given material to read and discuss in group and private sessions which pertains to this area. Furthermore, at least once in his work with the students, the counselor asks each individual if he thinks that his knowledge in this area is adequate; if it is not, the defect is investigated and provided for.

5. **Health Service.** Each student must have an annual physical check and bring the report of the same to the principal's office. No student may engage in school athletics without the written approval of parents. A physician is always on the bench for football games, and cooperation from the nearby hospital is very good. A physician visits the infirmary several times a week. The college infirmary with its full-time infirmarian is always at the disposal of the school for first aid treatment and cure of minor ailments. The health service is administered by the principal and the prefect of discipline.

6. **Discipline.** A strict "discipline" in the sense of orderliness is a characteristic of the school and it is precisely for this reason that many parents send their boys to it. The students come to school neatly dressed. Care of this matter rests primarily in the hands of the prefect of discipline. He keeps a check on lateness and absence. If a student is absent in the morning, the parents are contacted immediately by telephone if possible. All the other members of the staff, except the student counselors, are considered custodians of discipline.

7. **Placement.** Placement is regarded as embracing the phase of the student's life which chronologically follows completion of high school. Over the years for most students in this school the next step is college; for others it is employment or the services. Much of the problem-solving and decision-making which is the concern of counseling centers around placement.

In a recent year of the 160 graduates, for the first time every student immediately attended college. Almost one half registered at the nearby Catholic college. Other favorite colleges were Notre Dame, Holy Cross, Georgetown and similar Catholic colleges. Five registered at "ivy league" colleges and ten at low-tuition city and state colleges. Three entered the service academies. Seven began seminary education. All the planning for advanced study was facilitated in some way by the counselors' efforts, particularly through the dissemination of information concerning educational and vocational information.

Many of the graduates received college scholarships. Three quarters of them obtained at least one grant, and some obtained more than one. The bulk of these scholarships were awarded by two states on the basis of competitive examinations. Other grants were received from colleges directly and from foundations. The guidance department regards itself as sharing in these achievements because it alerted the junior and senior classes to the availability of most of these grants and in certain cases directed individual students to special awards for which they had particular qualifications.

PART II: THE EVALUATION

The literature on the evaluation of guidance programs is lengthy but unsatisfactory, as Patterson [3] points out. The essential difficulty with attempts to evaluate guidance programs is that of the criterion problem. The criterion problem is that just as there is disagreement among educators concerning the objectives of education in general, there is not "any generally accepted set of criteria for evaluating guidance." [4] For instance, counselee satisfaction as based upon student opinion has been used by some but rejected by others as an adequate method of evaluating guidance programs. The same may be said of student grades, cessation of "dropouts", entry into college or other educational institutions and the like. Criticism can be directed at these and other norms of evaluation.

Though the use of a single criterion may be rejected in evaluation, a single question addressed to a particular school should precede any examination of a guidance program. The question is: "What are you trying to accomplish through your guidance program?" The judgment that can be made concerning the school's guidance program must follow the investigation of the thoroughness with which its goals are pursued, provided, of course, its goals are acceptable. Hence, the procedure which will be used here will be an investigation of the school's goals in guidance and of the means used to achieve these goals. The data provided in Part I will be analyzed to determine the goals and the means used to fulfill them.

Evaluation connotes not only an estimate regarding one's doing something, but also a judgment concerning how well he is doing it. There are quantitative as well as qualitative aspects to evaluation. Thus in this evaluation a judgment will be made not only concerning whether work is being done in the necessary areas but an over-all rating of Superior, Good, Average, Poor, Inferior will be assigned.

The Objectives of Guidance in the School

From the listing of the various types of services offered the students in the school, as described in Part I, it is clear that the guidance department is interested in all aspects of the young person's life: academic, vocational, social, physical, religious. Realizing, then, that the student's total activity is embraced by the program, the goal of guidance could be summarized in this school as "personalized assistance to students concerning a wide variety of *transitional, situational,* and *developmental* problems and assistance." [5] This type of approach allows for breadth of view and scope of work and does not prevent depth in some areas. At the conclusion of the examination, an overall rating seems to be required because of the breadth embraced by the objectives of guidance in this school. It would be simpler to utilize a single criterion among those suggested, but such a choice would not include the total activity of the guidance program.

The Guidance Staff

The qualifications which the different members of the guidance staff bring to their work must be first examined.

The two guidance counselors have attended two summer institutes. Presuming that they obtained three graduate credits at each institute (the usual amount), their academic preparation seems to be quite deficient. Many states have two levels of certification—permanent certification which requires thirty academic credits in guidance and counseling, and provisional certification which requires about fifteen. Thus the counselors in this school do not come close to achieving the preparation which is demanded for state certification.

It happens that many states do not require that the guidance counselors in private schools be certified. Many counselors in these schools, nonetheless, have obtained certification because they believe that the training that precedes certification is mandatory for those who function in a professional capacity. They also are convinced that workers in private schools should be qualified to be hired in the public schools.

The guidance counselors might regard their religious convictions, ideals and training as substitutes for the professional courses which precede certification as guidance counselors. However, they would not regard this training as an adequate preparation for teaching, or becoming a social worker or psychiatrist. Just as special knowledge and skills are required for these other professional activities, they are also needed for guidance and counseling.

Before assigning an evaluation to the guidance staff, it should be profitable to reflect on the qualifications of counselors in one area—New York State, outside of New York City. In that area in 1964 it was learned that 98% of the full-time guidance counselors in 2,467 positions are certified by the New York State Education Department. [6] Hence certification and the training that precedes it has been achieved in many schools.

The guidance staff, therefore, deserves a rating of Inferior in academic training. This means that they make a poor start, but they could be Superior in practice through their knowledge and skill which are achieved through non-academic channels.

A note on the organization of the program through the cooperation of class teachers seems appropriate. The use of the term "permissive" with regard to the administration's attitude concerning teachers' group guidance activities may really indicate unconcern. Certainly the fact that only ten percent of the faculty professedly use group guidance procedures does not show faculty response to the permissiveness in this area. If the administration is convinced of the need for guidance, a stronger position would be likely to be taken. A program of group guidance considerations would be urged and a definite time put aside for the group guidance activity.

The rating for the relationship between the faculty and the administration with regard to guidance: Inferior.

1. **Admission of students.** This program is administered by the principal. In many other schools the guidance department either assumes complete responsibility for this work or assists the principal in the many chores which pertain to it. In general, however, it seems to be correct for this function to remain in the domain of the principal since it is an administrative task. Of course, the guidance department should remain involved in certain aspects of admissions. For instance, there should be an annual evaluation of the entry group in comparison with other groups of students.

No rating is required for this area.

2. **Orientation and adjustment of new students.** The orientation consists of two items (the Bulletin of Information and the letter about the first week's program) being sent to the parents and group guidance talks and discussions during the first few weeks of school. For the sake of academic adjustments, the parents of the first year students have the opportunity of visiting teachers at the beginning of the term.

Some observations seem to be called for. First, it would be better to begin the orientation to the new school at an earlier time than just before class starts. The new students could be invited to the school in May or June and at that time the orientation could be initiated. Second, no provision is made for the orientation of new students in the upper years. A definite program for these youths is as necessary as it is for the first year students. Finally, there is a need for more printed matter than the Bulletin of Information for the proper induction of the new students into their new life. Many schools publish a student handbook which contains far more information about the school than does the Bulletin of Information. It is recommended that the school publish such a handbook.

Rating: Good.

3. **Student records, academic and non-academic.** There is considerable overlapping in the records kept at this school. A file containing objective data is kept for each student in the principal's office, in the prefect of discipline's office and in the student counselor's office. This overlapping must be a source of wasted energy, time and money. It is recommended that there be a single records office and that the cumulative record of each student be securely kept in this office. It may still be necessary to maintain smaller confidential files about some students in one or other of the offices. But this type of file will normally be needed for very few students and need not contain a repetition of data on hand in the cumulative record folder.

At present the main folder on each student in the principal's office "may be seen by teachers upon request." This arrangement carries overtones which should not characterize students' records. The request must be made of the principal or of the registrar. When a request must be made, one does not have the right to what is requested. Yet teachers are told that they have an obligation to know and understand their students. It would seem that they have an equal right to the normal means for fulfilling that obligation—an unquestioned, and unrequested review of the material in the students' cumulative folder. A routine should be established whereby teachers have immediate access to these records without intermediaries. Of course, if the administrator learns that someone is abusing this right, he should be taken aside and admonished individually.

Rating: Average.

4. **Counseling. Educational.** All of the professional staff makes contributions in this area and this is fitting. It is possible, however, that not enough provision is made for individual differences in the program of the school. Outside of warning him, what is done for the failing student? Is tutoring regularly provided for without charge? May a student who has the ability and the desire for four years of science take that type of course? May a student who has aptitudes for many other subjects but little for foreign languages obtain all his credits in his best areas? In this school, at present the answer is negative to all these questions. Hence, the areas of choice for students in their educational counseling in the high school are quite limited. It is recommended that more choices be made available in line with the current recognition of the importance of individual differences.

"The student's fourth year interview is largely concerned with his vocational and educational planning." The implication here is that there is only one interview in the senior year. Provision should be made for a guidance interview at least every term and better still several times a term. Otherwise the counseling is concerned only with helping during a crisis, and it should be an integral element in the process of education. Furthermore, vocational and educational planning should be considered long before the fourth year. Discussion of these plans should be carried on throughout the four years in school. It is true that final plans should be examined in greater depth sometime in the fourth year but this will be more realistic and profitable when it is the climax of earlier discussions.

Vocational. The program for the background to vocational counseling is Superior.

Personal. This element of the guidance programs is clearly superior. Students have freedom of choice and yet techniques and activities are presented which provide an integrated view of life. The religious program offers activities which can satisfy many of the psychological human needs. It includes the supernatural bases for living as well as the natural. Thus all problems of living are considered. No important elements are omitted as too controversial. For instance, sex instruction is not feared and therefore neglected. It is approached by many professional members of the faculty from the religious, scientific and counseling viewpoints.

The sacraments and retreats are correctly viewed as elements of the guidance program. Guidance is concerned with choices in life, and the sacraments and retreats provide opportunity par excellence for making choices.

While the point might have been discussed under the "Guidance Staff" above, it seems equally appropriate to introduce as a special aspect of the guidance program of this school at this point—the fact that the religious as well as the general guidance and counseling functions are exercised by the same individuals. In the past decade the guidance movement went through a period during which educational and occupational counseling was separated and performed by different specialized individuals. Now the general trend is to unite various aspects of counseling on the premise that it is the single, undivided person who needs the counseling. Hence, if possible, where no special problems are to be dealt with, the counseling should be in the hands of one counselor. The same approach seems reasonable with regard to religious counseling. Of course, there are certain limiting factors. Briefly, this combination of counseling activity cannot be achieved if trained counselors are not available and if the size of the school mandates specialized counselors. However, specialized counselors require specialized training. If a counselor is appointed to work in the area of religious counseling, he must take courses and/or read extensively concerning counseling and the general educational scene as well as in his specialty. For instance, an untrained "priest-counselor" in a school may not be even approaching his full potential in assisting students as compared to the priest who has obtained a professional education in counseling.

Rating: Superior.

5. **Health Service.** In this area the guidance department in its concern for fulfilling the different needs of students must urge that health facilities and check-ups are available. It should also see to it that information about these services is imparted to students. However, it is a wise arrangement that others supervise the service.

Rating: none is required in this area.

6. **Discipline.** An incomplete view of the meaning of discipline seems to prevail in this school. Stress on "orderliness," "neatness," lateness. and absence connotes exclusive concern with the externals of conduct. A complete view of discipline embraces both the inner and outer life of the person. Hence, a divorce of the counselors from the involvement in discipline is an error. Roeber [7] shows that the counselor should be able to assist the faculty as a consultant on behavior. And Williamson [5] demonstrates that the counselor should also be a rehabilitation agent for students who have behavioral problems. Furthermore, the counselor attempts to assist the students to increase their self-understanding. Self-understanding pertains to one's behavior in all it's aspects; it certainly includes censured activity. Hence, instead of being exempted from this type of work the guidance workers should become involved with the program in its counseling aspects.

Rating: Average.

7. **Placement.** The imposing statistics concerning the graduates leave the observer with several questions. Some of these are the following. Is it necessarily a good sign that all graduates attend college or some equivalent type of advanced education institution? Is it not likely that at least a few of the 160 graduates would profit by a year or two of maturing in the world of paid or unpaid employment? Is it possible that the counselors and the administrators in the school are so report-minded that they assume too directive methods in counseling that freedom in this regard is effectively minimized? The individual differences that exist among so large a group of graduates, even though they were all in college preparatory courses, would seem to require that not all of them attend to their advanced training the September that follows graduation. Perhaps it would be wiser for schools to cite

for a given year the percentage who were graduated from college four or five years after high school graduation. Yet few schools offer these statistics.

The scholarship picture at this school looks good on the surface. Of course, in analyzing a school's scholarship record, there are many unanswered questions. For instance, how many of the students are underachievers who did not distinguish themselves in scholarship examinations? We also do not know if there were some students who were ill on scholarship examination days and were thereby eliminated from the competition. And then there are a few students who will do well in all examinations except the scholarship examination. We also ask how many students are accepting scholarships who do not need them and are thereby equivalently depriving others of a college education

Rating: Superior.

An overview of the guidance services of the school vis-a-vis the school's guidance objectives follows. This was regarded as personalized assistance regarding developmental decisions. In the seven areas that were examined one question that arises is: how many students are actually assisted, as opposed to the mere existence of general processes which were rated above. From the fact that the complete program exists and that students are regularly interviewed, it is clear that all students profit in some way from the proffered assistance. The second question that arises in the final overview is: how well are the students assisted? When faced with this question we recognize the difficulty of obtaining data with which to make the evaluation. And the question becomes changed to: How good are the counselors? Only a clinical judgment can be offered. That judgment is that, although the counselors began with an inadequate background, they were able to raise their program and its functioning to a high level. The final rating for the guidance program is: Superior. When the school was evaluated for accreditation purposes, the visiting experts concurred in this judgment.

REFERENCES

(1) Andrew, D. C. and Willey, R. D. *Administration and Organization of the Guidance Program.* New York: Harper and Brothers, 1958.

(2) Cribbin, J., Harris, P., and McMahon, Rev. W. *Insight* series. New York: Harcourt, Brace and World, 1963.

(3) Patterson, C. H. Program Evaluation. *Review of Educational Research*, Vol. 33, April 1963, 214-222.

(4) Miller, C. H. *Foundations of Guidance*. New York: Harper and Row, 1961, p. 405.

(5) Williamson, E. G. *Counseling Adolescents*. New York: McGraw-Hill, 1951, p. 219.

Williamson, E. G. The Fusion of Discipline and Counseling in the Educative Process. *Personnel and Guidance Journal*, Vol. 34, 1955, 74-79.

(6) Bureau of Guidance, New York State Education Department. *Guidance Personnel Trends*. 1964, p.1.

(7) Roeber, E. C. *The School Counselor*. Washington, D. C.: The Center for Applied Research in Education, 1963.

PANEL DISCUSSION

The panel discussion at the conclusion of the institute is charac-terized by the attempt to attend to problems which were judged to be important but which were not discussed earlier. In addition, re-curring themes were underlined. The Director of the Institute (Dr. Loughran) and the three workshop directors (Miss Ewell, Sr. M. Thomas, and Fr. Hennessy) were the members of the panel. Their main topics were: the counselor's public relations, the counselor's contacts with administration, the importance of feedback, the problem of defining the counselor's role, the counselor and teachers, and final-ly, some suggestions for the professional growth of the counselor.

DR. LOUGHRAN: In our panel discussion we would like to talk about some of the areas of the counselor's responsibil-ities which we had not covered earlier or had not given a great deal of emphasis to. For example, although we have concern about the professional growth of the counselor, that topic has not been comprehensively covered.

Another area which deserves our attention is the public relations responsibility of every counselor. Cer-tainly the director of guidance ought to be able to interpret the guidance program to all faculty members, to administration, to parents and to the community. Suppose we start with the public relations responsibility of the counselor. To begin the discussion, I should like to ask a question of the panel.

Do you believe that the counselor is responsible for the interpretation of the guidance program to the public? Is public relations a part of his job?

SR. M. THOMAS: I think it is part of the counselor's responsi-bility to make the aviliable services known to the ad-ministration, to the faculty and to the parents. Now I do not know how much that would involve public relations. I think that in so far as we are going to try to help the students and these people whom I just mentioned are all concerned with the students, then they have a right to know what we are trying to do.

DR. LOUGHRAN: But how does the counselor nterpret his role to the principal? Sister, you had to start out a grass roots program. There had not been any formalized guidance program in your school. What steps did you take, first of all, to impress the principal with the need for a guidance program and then to make it worthwhile for her to release you from your teaching time, to provide you with a very luxurious office—incidentally, Sister has a very lovely office—with the wherewith to decorate that office and furnish it? How did you sell your program to your principal?

SR. M. THOMAS: Well, since you were involved in it, and helped, I think you know the answer. But for the benefit of those who do not know, I think, first, the job of guidance counselor is to prove his or her value to the whole school, to try to make herself known as someone who can be of service, both to the principal and to the faculty. I began, by issuing a series of bulletins to the faculty, trying to impress upon them the need, by way of the services that we were *not* giving to the students and which really everyone recognized as necessary for the students. I think I stated there that if we wanted them to become competent and wholesome members of the Mystical Body, then our job was to reach each of them individually. But how could a teacher who had, say, a teaching load of 200 students, get to know each of them individually without any of the techniques that guidance would provide, like the cumulative record and the interview that the counselor would have with each student individually. They all saw the need; this was evident when fourteen out of the twenty-four we then had on the faculty signed up for one of the programs we asked them to participate in, like testing, records, occupational information, and group guidance. They volunteered their services.

DR. LOUGHRAN: Father, you had a somewhat similar problem. Did you handle this differently?

FR. HENNESSY: I walked into a very favorable position. But I would say that about eight years before I was the full-time student counselor, one of my predecessors had a a big problem about how to convince the principal that he should be full-time at the task. He did have a public relations job. I think he succeeded more by the method of reasoning, than anything else. The principal realized that the guidance man was put in a position that was somewhat contradictory if he were both teaching and counseling. In other words, he'd be assigning grades to the students and he'd be in a disciplinary situation, if he were teaching. Ultimately, the principal accepted the fact that he should be a full-time in counseling. So his work was, primarily, getting across to the principal this image, (to borrow a term from public relations) of what the counselor should be. He was successful there and I fell heir to this particular benefit. I think there is a constant problem of public relations, however. You can fall heir to a good situation and then sit back and retire. If the administration and especially the students don't realize that you are working at your job, you get back to the situation that existed ten, fifteen or twenty years ago.

DR. LOUGHRAN: This is exactly what we are talking about. How do you let the admnistration, and the teaching staff, and the parents, and the community know that you really are working? That you are not sitting in an air-conditioned office?

MISS EWELL: I think probably here is an area where the counselor himself is the best public relations. I do not like the word public relations. I like "interpreter of the guidance program." If you are the counselor in a school who concerns yourself with students all the time, the staff perceives of you as working with students. If the parents of the children only see you when their child has had a problem, the parents begin to conceive of you

as a person who deals with problems. It is our actions
that tend to interpret our role. And I think as counselors
we have a real responsibility to see that our actions
interpret the kind of role that we want to have interpreted. Now there are times when we are forced into
taking a kind of role which we as counselors feel is not
good. This is a difficult kind of a situation. And here I
think you have to approach the people with whom you
are working. And I think you have to look at the person
you are trying to interpret to and interpret so that it
has meaning for that person. After all you are all counselors. This is what you are trained to do. You have to
get into the perceptual field of this person. If you are
working as I did at one time for a superintendent who
was only interested in dollars and cents, then you may
have to interpret values in terms of dollars and cents.
If you are working with a staff that is interested in
students' development, then you interpret your role so
that they begin to see in terms of their frame of reference. And I do not think that this is a sneaky way of
doing it.

DR. LOUGHRAN: Very often counselors complain that they do
not have the time to do very much counseling, that they
do not have the time to run the kind of occupational
information for the students that they would like to run
because of the clerical burden that has been placed upon them by the principal. The principal makes them
responsible for scheduling, for example, and the complete scheduling problem is dumped into the counselor's lap. This is a very heavy clerical chore. How does
this counselor interpret his role to a principal when the
principal issues a fiat? "This is your responsibility. I am
giving you this duty—this nice little plum. You can do
all the clerical work for me." The counselor becomes
an administrative assistant rather than a counselor.
How does the counselor feel about that?

MISS EWELL: I'll react to that. If your administrator issues an
order, you'd better obey. Those are just the facts of
life. However, if you are going to bring about change,

then I think you are going to have to help your administrator make a decision. Now, again, I think this goes back to your administrator, and no one method, no one technique is going to be workable with every administrator or superior with whom you work. But, there are a number of devices which I have seen successfully used. One, I think, was mentioned yesterday —and I think it is something we neglect—that is, an annual report. Now we like to say that everything is bright and rosy but I think as counselors our annual report should not stress so much the wonderful things we are doing. It should stress some of the big needs that we see that are not being met and some of the reasons why they are not being met. You are then giving your administrators some information which they probably never thought about. Now I visit schools constantly during the year. I am probably in and out of about a hundred schools and I would guarantee you that as I sit down with the principal and the counselor at the end of my visit, in 25 percent or more of those schools the administrator will turn to the counselor and say, "Why didn't you tell me this?" Now maybe they had attempted to and it didn't get through. Maybe you have to bring somebody in from the outside if that is the way to get the attention. Maybe you have to put it on a dollar and cents basis; maybe you have to indicate areas of need. You have to find the way that your administrator can understand and gradually you will find, I am sure, a reinterpretation of your role and what you are doing. But this, to me, is one of the major responsbilities of the counselor to the guidance program. It is what I like to call the leadership role. You are the person who understands the guidance program and what it should be. You are responsible for acquainting your administrator with this in a way that he or she will accept, in a way that has meaning for the local situation in which this person finds himself.

SR. M. THOMAS: May I add something to that? Talking about this report to administrators, I found it very helpful when beginning the guidance program to have our faculty committee chairmen write up what had taken place during the year and then I handed it to our administrator at the end of the year. This is when the program was still only in then planning stages, when nothing really concrete had happened yet. It lets your administrator in on the ground floor and I think it really creates a very favorable impression. I admit I was a little disheartened when I saw my administrator's shoes on top of it a couple of weeks after I'd given it to her but I think she read it first, because she was very amenable to the program afterwards.

FR. HENNESSY: I wish to react to the problem of the principal's foisting administrative work on the guidance counselor. When you earlier posed the question regarding the way to convince the principal about the importance of guidance, I first thought of a sit-down strike, then picketing, but somehow I do not think that they would be so successful. But I do think that it is important that the counselor have a long-range view. He may not succeed in getting relieved of some of these administrative functions in one year, but if he definitely starts a campaign of attempting to convince his local administrator he will succeed ultimately as long as he is secure in his own position. When you can go with a clear head to the administratior and say, "Look, the authorities in the field are urging that the compiling of many reports and recommendations to colleges is not the counselor's kind of work." If you do feel secure and maintain a steady position, ultimately you will win out. You have to make sure that you are looking to the future. It's not enough for you to try once and say, "Well, now he knows my position" and that is the end,—oh, no, you have to keep trying,—another year, another term, and the principal or administrator might change his position.

DR. LOUGHRAN: I think you have put your finger on very important points. So often the guidance counselor tries to do this job of interpretation alone, and then I think he becomes an administrator, not a guidance counselor. Sometimes the guidance work is a cooperative venture, but too often it's a battle, a conflict of interest. The principal has responsibility for the conduct of the total school, and it looks as though the guidance counselor is fighting a long battle in the interest of the guidance program and somehow or other, the students get lost in the shuffle. The more that the counselor can enlist the services of every other person on the faculty who can possibly be involved in interpreting the guidance program, the stronger the guidance program is and the least conflict of interest there is with the administrator. If you have three math teachers who are heart and soul with you on some aspects of your program and if they make their appreciation of the guidance program known to the administrator, this is interpretation from a different point of view and doesn't look as though you with your vested interest are trying to blow your own horn. Somebody else is appreciating what is being done. I think the more you can decentralize the interests of the guidance program, spread them around, so that every other faculty member who is at all favorably disposed, can become involved, the better your guidance program will be.

MISS EWELL: May I just mention one other thing here that I think is extremely important. And that is that the counselor is only one part of the total school program, and the counselor also has to understand the administrator's problem. And I think as a good counselor you can not look only at your program; you have to see the total school program. And I think this is something we constantly have to keep in mind. I believe that there are very general and real reasons why your administrator is not able to progress as rapidly as you think he or she might, and you ought to understand and appreciate the position of the administrators. I think we ought not to become such specialists that we look only at our own little narrow field and keep our blinders on.

DR. LOUGHRAN: I can think of a guidance counselor who is not too far away from me whose administrator is about seventy-eight years old and who has a very large school and many problems on her shoulders and the guidance counselor did initially what Father just said, sent a memo reminding the administrator that this and this was needed and then said, "Well, I let her know." But you can't do this. You have to hammer away at it. You invent creative ways of interpreting to the administrator, reminding the administrator, not nagging, not dinning, but arousing her interest. Ultimately she can't stand being reminded and she has to do something about it and you usually get what you want . . . I think we can't spend too much time on this.

We have opened up some ideas for you to think about. If some of you have questions on this area of leadership, interpretation, responsibility of guidance counselors, let's see if we can answer them.

QUESTION: We have talked about the service of the guidance program to students, the service of the guidance program to other members of the faculty, but we have not said very much about what is our role in relation to the principal's responsibility for running a school. What does the guidance program contribute to the administrator?

MISS EWELL: I think here is the crux of the whole thing. Now there are a number of ways I think you can assist. For instance, one of the first ways that immediately comes to mind is in the whole matter of scheduling. As a counselor you can become very much involved in this area and provide your administrator with a great deal of help in developing his program. I think you can do a great deal in providing statistical information about groups of pupils. The administrator very often is interested in this information. For instance, the results coming from a follow-up study which may have implications for curriculum would be interesting to the administrator. Certainly, information about the students who are dropping out of school—what kind of pupils are being lost and why. We, as counselors, have this kind of information. I think it is a matter of digesting it and putting it in the form that will help the principal. Then I think, of course, that we often can act as a consultant to the administrator. In the matter of working with parents, I once worked with a principal who, when an irate parent would come in, would say, "Let's go over to the guidance office and talk with Miss Ewell." And in getting the parent into the guidance office we could then do counseling with this person and I would assume a role. We used to joke, the principal and I. I used to say I could always tell by the way he asked me whether I was free, what sort of role I was to play, and I played a variety of roles which enabled him to handle the situation. Now I think this is a perfectly legitimate service for guidance, but of course this needs deep understanding between you and your administrator.

DR. LOUGHRAN: I think we often forget our responsiblity to feed back. I don't know how many times I have talked to high school principals who will say, "95 per cent of our boys go on to college, 90 per cent of our girls go on to college," and they almost never know how many last beyond sophomore year in college. But this is something that the guidance counselor can contribute. The guidance counselor who does follow-up studies might say, "Surely, 95 per cent were admitted to college, but only 30 per cent of them lasted through sophomore year in college," and maybe could say that the school was not meeting the needs of its students for adequate preparation in this area versus this area. I can give you another very simple illustration. One of our schools had a high proportion of students who have foreign parentage, both Italian and French. At that time the students were administered the American Council on Education Psychological Test, which had Q scores and L scores, quantitative scores and language scores. The total scores for these students were fine, but there was a considerable differential between the scores achieved in the language area versus those achieved in the numerical area. This simple bit of information was shared with the administrator and he was able to call in his teachers and say, "Look, we are doing a beautiful job in math and science, but let's take a look at the lack of our ability to up-grade the youngsters in their verbal skill." Very simple. And yet we do so little feedback though this role that the guidance program should play with administration.

QUESTION: Maybe by bringing certain situations to the notice of the principal, who in turn may bring them to the attention of those in higher authority, eventually something might be done.

FR. HENNESSY: Yes, if we get the whole chain of command alerted to problems through feedback, this would be helpful. However, we may be dealing here with situations in which guidance and administration are overlapping. I see three problems here. First, both the principal and the counselor may both be very information-minded; hence they may both be independently gathering the information; and the opposite situation may exist where neither is doing this work. Secondly both may regard it as his prerogative to be the feedback specialist to all members of the staff; and again the opposite situation may obtain such that hardly anyone knows much about what's going on. And third, the feedback and information-gathering aspect of the counselor's job may pyramid such that he is putting this information to use constantly but in tasks extraneous to his counseling. I have an uncomfortable feeling that some counselors are pleased to take on these chores because they recognize that by doing them well they are thereby impressing the administration, as they are. But meanwhile the individuals are not being counseled and the guidance program suffers. Can we say that all these functions, as for instance those that Miss Ewell was mentioning, are primary functions of the counselor?

MISS EWELL: Can we say anythng is the primary function? What is your primary function may not be mine. I do not think that any activity can legitimately be called a primary activity of a counselor. There are certain situations in which, for instance, if you had only two periods a day for guidance, and you have a thousand students, the one-to-one relationship is pretty weak. Maybe, I say only maybe, you as a counselor in that situation might better spend your time in doing some of these things which would affect a large group of students than in putting a great deal of emphasis on helping the one or two. I am thinking here of guidance rather than strictly counseling, because I think these are guidance services. Naturally, if you are in a school system where you are fortunate enough to have a Director of Research, this is a guidance service which the Director of Research would handle. If you happen to have a Vice Principal who is statistically minded, it would be that. The role of the counselor fluctuates, and a great deal depends, I think, upon your load, your definite assignment, the feelings of the administrator.

FR. HENNESSY: I agree that in practice the function of the counselor varies with local conditions.

QUESTION: You've been usng the word, "counselor." A counselor counsels students, doesn't he? When you use counselor for guidance, isn't that a misuse of the word?

MISS EWELL: Not in my definition. Now I am talking about a counselor in a secondary school. He works with the guidance program of services. He has a number of different functions or roles which he performs, of which counseling is one technique which is needed.

QUESTION: Then he shouldn't be called a counselor; he called a guidance-person because "counselor" suggests something.

MISS EWELL: And I think that many authorities agree with you. This is one of the things that Mr. Shear brought up, I think, and you do find a number of people using it. The word counselor now is beginning, in the secondary school to mean, quite something different than a counselor in a school of higher education. The American School Counselor Association, the ASCA, in

1964 issued its Statement of Policy for Secondary School Counselors. This statement and accompanying documents will help us to get common terminology and a common understanding of the role and function of the school counselor. As far as I am concerned, the secondary school counselor uses counseling as only one of many techniques for the fulfillment of his functions. And guidance is a much broader area to which the administrators and teachers and many people contribute, the counselor contributing a professional role.

QUESTION: But if we're not guiding students we're not doing our jobs. Is all the guiding done in the guidance office in a one-to-one relationship?

MISS EWELL: For instance, I as a counselor work with students in post high school education and planning, and I find I help them choose colleges fairly well, but when they get to college they come back to me and say, "But my English,—I am not prepared for the English." This is for me to let the administrator know—not to revamp the English. I become an information-giver. And it may be that at that point, my time might best be spent in gathering together this information, which might affect all the students in the school for the next four years or beyond. I think that this is where too often counselors err. We are going to have to know where we can work most effectively.

SR. M. THOMAS: I think the greatest percentage of our time should be spent in direct service to the students. This is what we are there for, to facilitate their growth and their self-direction. I know that Miss Ewell has a definite point here because we have to be ready to spend some time in giving information to our principals, and to the teachers but I think the greatest percentage of our time should be used for counseling. Probably the questioner is objecting to the use of the word "counselor" out of the context of "direct service to the students."

DR. LOUGHRAN: But I do not think there is a misuse of the term guidance counselor. Mathewson wrestled with this whole matter of the terminology and for a time he felt that there should be a hierarchy within the school guidance program, with the school counselor being part of this hierarchy. Whether the guidance worker came above or below the school counselor was never quite clear, because Mathewson began to appreciate that the school counselor is a professional educator and not a technician. The guidance worker could be someone who might plan the career conference program and invite all the speakers and write the thank-you letters, and this would be a technical part of a person's responsibility. But the professional educator has to be somebody who can work with other professional educators and he must be a school counselor. He has to have this professional identity even though some of his jobs might be a clerical operation. Your doctor is no less a medical man because he has to jot down information on your chart. He is still a professionally trained individual with highly professional responsibility and school counselors may have these minor technical assignments which are essential to the operation of his profession.

SR. M. THOMAS: Don't you think then, Dr. Loughran, that the guidance counselor would have to sit down and figure out in terms of percentage, how much time he is going to give to this?

DR. LOUGHRAN: This is a big responsibility of the school counselor, to figure out the allocation of time, how much time will be given to collecting information and seeing that the cumulative records are really well managed and handled, how much time to the one-to-one relationship, how much time to the training of other teachers for a group guidance responsibility, how much time to working with the parents or working with the administrator. The counselor can not do this unless he has a pretty good picture of his own professional self concept, and his professional self concept is, "In which way am I most effective in terms of the responsibility of my job in *this* situation, in *this* school, with *this* administrator?" I know some of you work in schools where the amount of time you need to give to the one-to-one relationship is very slim, because you have a highly trained faculty whose training has fitted them, too, to the one-to-one relationship for most of the problems that young people have. And your responsibility might be for those problems in depth and not necessarily for all the problems of all young-sters. A great deal of your time might be used in consultation, as the resource person for that faculty. And I know of other schools where the counselor is going to spend almost all of his time in the one-to-one relationship because the problems are so heavy and so burdensome, and there isn't anyone else who can do this and perhaps the administrator can handle all of these other activities through the administrative assistant or through a faculty committee.

MISS EWELL: Part of the solution is whether you want to be the one who is greasing the squeaky wheel or whether you want to develop a program which will prevent squeaky wheels. You find that there is a wide variation. A person going into a beginning counseling program may spend the first three months without ever seeing a student. I know of a counselor who did this and he has one of the soundest guidance programs now. Why? Because he didn't know anything about the students, anything about the school, and he had to get some of this information before he could be very helpful. And he took about the first few months just to do some of this—then moved into the guidance. I think this is a highly flexible thing. There is no one pattern that fits everybody and every single school.

DR. LOUGHRAN: The big difficulty is that guidance counselors, particularly those who have been too long in the system without being professionally self-critical, permit themselves to have their duties and responsibilities grow like hop seed because they do not want to sit down and think through what their real role is. And beginning counselors too often are afraid that they will not be accepted by the faculty and by administration if they do not do all the things that they are asked to do. They have no real inner security about what their professional role is in the school. If they had this they could do the clerical work without worrying about it because they know ultimately they will be able to interpret what their real role is and they will be able to slide out of this or get some other people to do some of the technical chores. Each of us has a responsibility to ourselves, to the role—expectation in that school, to the services we can render to students, and to our profession, to be certain that we know what it is that the guidance program should accomplish. And I think that this is why we spend so much time in this institute talking about the goals of the guidance program. If you know what the goals of the program are, then perhaps you can begin to see how you fit in to the accomplishing of these goals as your program moves along.

We have a responsibility to evaluate the contribution of the guidance program to the school. In doing so, we may stumble on the knowledge that the curriculum is not providing an adequate preparation to the students' plans. For example, you may come from an area where your school is a feeder school for a local college. The curriculum in your school may not be preparing youngsters so that they can adequately progress in that college. May you as a guidance counselor feel that the curriculum is none of your business? It is part of your business. And you have a responsibility to interpret what it is you are learning to your curriculum committee and to your administration. You have an obligation, I think, to disperse this kind of information among faculty, if the administration is not doing very much about it.

FR. HENNESSY: There is another kind of information which the counselor may have the opportunity to bring to the attention of teachers. I refer to recent advances in university course work and the many scholarships that go along with the new courses. For instance, there are many National Science Foundation awards for teachers; such announcements may come to the counselor's office that might not be received by other members of the staff. Sometimes we can tell a teacher that there are outstanding facilities in a particular university and can mention the scholarship opportunities. Perhaps something can be accomplished in that way.

DR. LOUGHRAN: We could spend just a few minutes on the professional growth of the counselor. Think of the counselor who is on the job, who is partially or fully trained and who has been on the job for a while, whose responsibility is continued professional growth. Whose responsibility is this? Is the counselor solely responsible? Does administration have the responsibility?

FR. HENNESSY: If you take the title that used to be used in many of the high schools—the headmaster, this would seem to imply first of all that the principal has the primary role of leadership, as an educator and as someone who should be fostering growth on the part of his staff. That would illustrate how the principal does have a responsibility in this area. He has a responsibility, I suggest, not only to encourage the professional growth by way of reading and so forth, but also by making opportunities available—namely enabling the counselor to get to meetings, and providing him with sufficient carfare and the like. The responsibility is not all up in the air, it's pretty much down to earth, too.

DR. LOUGHRAN: I have an axe to grind as some of you might well have recognized. Some of you do not get enthusiastic about professional affiliations. And I think that this is one field in which you must be active, because the field is so dynamic and changes so rapidly, and because otherwise you as counselors will be working in professional isolation. Very often there is no other counselor on the staff. If you are a teacher, there are very many other teachers on the staff. You have an opportunity to discuss your classroom problems, your teaching problems with other teachers, and get some new thinking on it. But as counselors, almost no one on the staff will speak your language, and if you are to stay up to date, if you are to grow professionally, you must have some kind of professional affiliation. There's a practical side to this, too. Accrediting bodies begin to look for the professional affiliations of those on their staff. When the Middle States comes into your school and reviews the guidance program, the evaluators want to know whether the guidance counselor is a member of the national professional association, the local professional associations, how many professional meetings he attends, etc. And so, from the practical point of view this is essential for your school, even if it were not essential for you, and it *is* essential for you. In terms of professional associations, you should be members and you should attend as many meetings as you are able to get to; you should be reading journal articles, too. Some of you may not be aware that there is a Personnel and Guidance association called APGA. Its address is 1605 New Hampshire Avenue, NW, Washington, D.C. 20009. It publishes *The Personnel and Guidance Journal*. The National Vocational Guidance largest division is the American School Counselors Association. Both of these divisions publish journals. NVGA publishes the *Vocational Guidance Quarterly*, ASCA publishes *The School Counselor*. Excellent Journals, with many practical suggestions to be used in the operation of you guidance program. For those of you who are with student personnel at the college level, there is the American College Personnel Association, another division of APGA. Some of you are interested in rehabilitation counseling, you work with exceptional children, those who have suffered from one or another type of physical handicap. There is the American Rehabilitation Counseling Association. Some of you are involved in teacher education. This is Student Personnel Association for Teacher Education. Most of you are not yet in or eligible for the Association (for Counselor Education and Supervision), although those of you who become community supervisors of guidance programs would be eligible for membership in ACES. All of you would be eligble for membership in APGA. You would not be eligible for professional membership, most of you, until you have acquired 60 graduate credits and a number of years of experience. But at least you can become a member at large. It entitles you to your professional journals which you will be forced to read because you have paid for them. There are local branches of these Associations, too. For instance, in New York area we have NYPGA. There is a Long Island Personnel and Guidance Association. There is a Westchester Personnel and Guidance Association. Also, many states have their own State Personnel and Guidance Association. These provide opportunities for you to meet with other professionally trained people. They will welcome you.

For many of you there are local Catholic guidance councils. There are some 35 of them throughout the United States. These give you an opportunity to meet with counselors in Catholic schools, on the problems that might be peculiar to the operation of the guidance program in your own school. Those of you in the Catholic Schools should certainly subscribe to the *National Catholic Guidance Conference Journal*. It can be ordered by writing to the Executive Director, 3600 S. Kinnickinnic Avenue, Milwaukee, Wisconsin 53207. It is a professional journal, of which all of us are very proud. The articles that are published in it are of a caliber that would be acceptable in any professional journal. It is a small journal. You can read it in an hour, most times. And then I hope you can go back and read some of the articles much more carefully because they may be very beneficial to you.

You can not get along without professional association. You should affiliate with some group that has the same professional concerns that you have. I have stressed APGA because our tendency is often to feel that if we belong to a local Catholic guidance conference that this satisfies our obligation for professional affiliation. It does not. Accrediting organizations demand national professional affiliation, and so, from this practical viewpoint alone you should become members of APGA.

Well, to speak now in terms of the whole institute I think some of our purposes were to open up avenues for exploration and for your thinking. We have tried during these days to indicate the complexity of the problems of the organization and administration of the guidance program. We hoped that you would not just take a look and feel it was easy. We might have made it all sound very difficult because we did not want you to be smugly self satisfied with whatever programs you have, and inclined to feel that if the programs were not meeting the needs of the students, it was the students' fault. We hope that you have had an opportunity to evaluate critically some of the programs that go on in your own school. We hope that we have encouraged you to do some self criticism in regard to your own programs and in regard to the role that you play in the guidance program in your own school or as a faculty member in the school. We hope we've made you ask yourself, "How much have I contributed to the development of the guidance services in my school?" We hope, too, that we have encouraged you to begin to take a look at the research literature in the field like experimental programs in terms of the design of a guidance program within a school. We hope that we have begun to provide a little "know how" for some of the beginners in the field so that you can begin to see ways in which you might want to move ahead.

A SCHOOL COUNSELOR'S LIBRARY

INTRODUCTION. *This list is meant to provide an answer to the school counselor's question, "What books should I have in my office or in my waiting room?" Of course, each counselor's situation differs, and special demands made on a counselor may require additional reference material. Nevertheless, it does seem that a minimum number of books for reference and frequent reading should be at hand for the working counselor. The list which follows may be of special assistance to those who are initiating a professional guidance service. Others may find it to be a convenient norm for upgrading their own present collection.*

For the convenience of counselors who face budgetary limitations, the cost of each item is listed. These costs are correct as of the date of going to press.

An asterisk (*) has been assigned to those books which in the judgment of the editor are of special importance for the daily work of the counselor. Hence, it is possible that some counselors may regard this listing as essentially the equivalent of two levels: the essential books (*) and the important ones.

For those who wish to examine the pattern and the limitations to the listing, the categories of the suggested publications and a possible system for the collection (A,1, etc.) follows:

A. *Educational Information*

    1. *College Data (Directories, Orientation, How to enter books, etc.)*

    2. *Other School Data (Directories, Orientation, How to enter books, etc., including secondary education.)*

    3. *Scholarship Information (all levels)*

    4. *Study Skills*

B. *Vocational Information*

    1. *General (Books on careers, career development)*

    2. *Books on specific careers, industries, etc.*

    3. *Brochures* (In a filing cabinet)

C. *Guidance and Counseling*

D. *Measurement*

E. *Program Management and Development (Organization and Administration)*

F. *Psychology*

G. *Education in General*

H. *Journals*

A. EDUCATIONAL INFORMATION

1. College Data

Accredited Higher Institutions. U.S. Office of Education, Bulletin No. 24. Washington, D.C.: Supt. of Documents, Government Printing Office, 1960 — $.60

American Junior Colleges. Washington, D.C.: American Council on Education, 1963 — $10.00

American Universities and Colleges. Washington, D.C.: American Council on Education, 1964 — $15.00

Barron's Guide to the Two Year Colleges. S. Eskow, Great Neck: N.Y.: Barron's Educational Series, Inc., 1966 — $3.50.

Catholic Colleges and Universities. Chicago, Ill. 60604: Catholic College Bureau, Room 626, 25 E. Jackson Blvd. (Free to guidance workers, principals, pastors, libraries; $1.50 to others.)

College Blue Book. 4 vols. Christian E. Burkel and associates. Yonkers-on-Hudson, N.Y.: The College Blue Book, 1965 $60.00 (set)

College Handbook. Princeton, N.J.: College Entrance Examination Board, 1965-67 — $2.50

Colleges and Specialized Schools and Colleges. 4th ed. Boston: Porter Sargent, 1964 — $6.00

Education Directory, Part 3: *Higher Education*. Washington, D.C.: Government Printing Office, annual — $1.00

Lovejoy's College Guide. Clarence E. Lovejoy. New York: Simon & Schuster, 1966 — cloth-$6.50; paper-$3.50

Manual of Freshman Profiles. Princeton, N.J.: College Entrance Examination Board, 1965-67 — $5.00

National Directory of Schools and Vocations. A. E. Miller and Betty I. Brown. Erie, Pa.: St. John Kanty Press, 1963 — $12.95

New American Guide to College. Gene R. Hawes. Columbia U. Press, 1966 — $8.95; Signet Pocketbook-$.95

Official Guide to Catholic Educational Institutions in the U. S. Rockville Centre, N.Y.: Catholic Institutional Directory Co.; Published in association with Department of Education, NCWC, annual — $3.95

Patterson's American Education. Mt. Prospect, Ill.: Patterson's Educational Directories, Inc., 1965 — $25.00

Patterson's Schools Classified. Mt. Prospect, Ill.: Patterson's Educational Directories, Inc., annual — $3.50

2. Other School Data (including secondary education)

Accredited Technical Institute Programs. New York: Engineers Council for Professional Development, annual — $.25

American Trade School Directory. Z. H. Croner. Queens Village, N.Y.: Croner Publications, 1964 (monthly changes announced) $12.00

Directory for Exceptional Children. Boston: Porter Sargent, 1962 — $6.00

Lovejoy's Vocational School Guide - A Handbook of Job Training Opportunities. New York: Simon and Schuster, 1965 — cloth-$5.95; paper-$2.95

Lovejoy's Prep School Guide. New York: Harper and Row, 1963 — cloth-$5.95; paper-$3.95

Private Independent Schools. Wallingford, Conn.: Bunting and Lynn, Inc., 1964 — $12.00

Technician Education Yearbook, 1963-64. Ann Arbor, Mich.: Prakken Publications, Inc. — $10.00

3.   Scholarship Information

Financial Assistance for College Students: Undergraduate: R.C. Mattingly. Washington: Government Printing Office. 1965 — $1.25

Lovejoy's Scholarship Guide. New York: Simon and Schuster, 1964 — cloth-$4.95; paper-$2.95

Need a Lift? The American Legion, Dept. S., P.O. Box 1055, Indianapolis, Ind. 46206, annual — $.25

National Register of Scholarships and Fellowships. Vol. 1, Register of Scholarships and Loans. New York: Regents Publishing Co., 1964 — $15.00

Scholarships, Fellowships and Loans. S. Norman Feingold. Cambridge, Mass.: Bellman Publishing Co., — Vol. 3 (1958)-$10.00; Vol. 4 (1962)-$10.00

4.   Study Skills

Reed, P., S.J. *Do It Right!* Bronx, N.Y.: Jesuit Educational Association, 1951 — $.50

Robinson, F. P. *Effective Study.* (rev. ed.) New York: Harper, 1961 — $4.50

Tussing, L. *Study and Succeed.* (college students). New York: Wiley, 1962 — $2.95

Weigand, G. *How To Succeed in High School.* Woodbury, N.Y.: Barrons — $.95

B.   VOCATIONAL   INFORMATION

1.   General

Dictionary of Occupational Titles. U. S. Employment Service. Superintendent of Documents, Government Printing Office, 1965 Vol. I, Definitions of Titles — $5.00
 *Vol. II, Occupational Classification — $4.25

Forrester, Gertrude. *Occupational Literature, an Annotated Bibliography.* (2nd ed.) New York: H. W. Wilson Co., 1964 — $6.50

Hoppock, R. *Occupational Information.* (2nd ed.) New York: McGraw-Hill, 1963—$7.95

*Norris, Wilma, Zeran, F. R. and Hatch, R. N. *The Informational Service in Guidance.* Chicago: Rand McNally, 1960 — $7.50

Occupational Outlook Handbook. U.S. Department of Labor. Washington: Superintendent of Documents, Government Printing Office, biennial—$5.00

Roe, Anne. *The Psychology of Occupations.* New York: Wiley, 1956 — $6.95

Super, D. E. *The Psychology of Careers.* New York: Harper, 1957 — $5.75

Where To Find Vocational Training in New York City. New York: Vocational Advisory Service, 1964 — $7.50

2.   Specific Careers, Industries

Some book publishers offer series of books on occupations. Among these publishers are:

> E. P. Dutton, New York (books on 14 careers)
> Julian Messner, New York (books on 40 careers)
> Richards Rosen Press, New York (books on 75 careers)
> Vocational Guidance Manuals, New York (books on 40 careers)

3. Brochures, Monographs, etc. (in filing cabinets)

Several publishers offer a series of this type of material. Among these publishers are:

> Occupational Monographs (4000-8000 words)
> > Bellman Publishing Company, Cambridge, Mass.
> > The Institute for Research, Chicago, Ill.

> Occupational Briefs (about 3000 words)
> > Careers, Largo, Fla. (Kit of 970 items—$97.50) — *Annual subscription*: $30.00
> > Chronicle Guidance Publications, Moravia, N.Y. — *Annual occupational subscription*: $30.00
> > Science Research Associates, Chicago, Ill. (Kit—$165) *Annual subscription*: $19.50

C. GUIDANCE AND COUNSELING

Belka, Brother Marion et al. *Being and Becoming.* Group Guidance Series. Milwaukee: Bruce, 1966. The first of the series of four is in print: *Encounter.* $1.35 (text); $2.00 (group leader's manual).

Cottle, W. C. and Downie, N. M. *Procedures and Preparation for Counseling.* Englewood Cliffs, N.J.: Prentice-Hall, 1960 — $7.95

Cribbin, J.J., Harris, P., and McMahon, W.J. *The Insight Series.* 4 books and teachers' handbooks (a group guidance program) New York: Harcourt, Brace & World, 1961. Set—$15.20

Curran, C. *Counseling in Catholic Life and Education.* New York: MacMillan, 1952 — $5.75

Driver, Helen et al. *Counseling and Learning through Small-Group Discussion.* Madison, Wisconsin: Monona Publications, 1958 — $7.00

*Glanz, E. *Foundations and Principles of Guidance.* Boston: Allyn and Bacon, 1964 — $7.50

Hagmaier, G. and Gleason, R. *Counselling the Catholic.* New York: Sheed and Ward, 1959 — $4.50

Mathewson, R. *Guidance Policy and Practice.* (3rd ed.) New York: Harper and Row, 1962 — $6.00

*McGowan, J. F. and Schmidt, L. D. *Counseling: Readings in Theory and Practice.* New York: Holt, Rinehart and Winston, 1962 — $7.95

Miller, C. H. *Foundations of Guidance.* New York: Harper and Row, 1961 — $6.00

Roeber, E. C. *The School Counselor.* Washington, D.C.: The Center for Applied Research in Education, 1963 — $3.95

*Rogers, C. *On Becoming a Person.* Boston: Houghton Mifflin, 1961 — $7.00

Traxler, A. and North, R. D. *Techniques of Guidance.* (3rd. ed.) New York: Harper, 1966 — $9.95

*Tyler, Leona. *The Work of the Counselor.* (2nd ed.) New York: Appleton-Century-Crofts, 1961 — $4.75

*Warters, Jane. *Techniques of Counseling.* (2nd. ed.) New York: MacMillan, 1964 — $7.95

*Williamson, E. G. *Vocational Counseling.* New York: McGraw-Hill, 1965 — $6.95

*Wrenn, C. G. *The Counselor in a Changing World.* Washington, D.C.: American Personnel and Guidance Association, 1962.

D. MEASUREMENT

Buros, O. K. *Tests in Print.* Highland Park, N.J.: Gryphon Press, 1961 — $7.00

Diederich, P. B. *Short-Cut Statistics for Teacher-Made Tests.* Princeton, N. J.: Educational Testing Service, 1960 — Free

*Froehlich, C. P. and Hoyt, K. B. *Guidance Testing.* Chicago: Science Research, 1960 — $5.25

Garrett, H. E. *Statistics in Psychology and Education.* New York: David McKay, 1958 — $5.50

Guilford, J. P. *Fundamental Statistics in Psychology and Education.* (4th ed.) New York: McGraw-Hill, 1965 — $8.50

Goldman, L. *Using Tests in Counseling.* New York: Appleton-Century-Crofts, 1961 — $7.00

Selltiz, Claire, et al. *Research Methods in Social Relations.* New York: Holt, Rinehart and Winston, 1959 — $6.20

Super, D. E. and Crites, J. O. *Appraising Vocational Fitness.* (rev. ed.) New York: Harper, 1962 — $8.75

E. PROGRAM MANAGEMENT AND DEVELOPMENT

(ORGANIZATION AND ADMINISTRATION)

Hatch, R.N. and Stefflre, B. *Administration of Guidance Services.* Englewood Cliffs, N.J.: Prentice-Hall, 1965 — $8.95

Ohlsen, M. E. *Guidance Services in the Modern School.* New York: Harcourt, Brace & World, 1964 — $7.25

Saalfeld, L. J. *Guidance and Counseling for Catholic Schools.* Chicago: Loyola, 1958 — $4.50

*Zeran, F. R. and Riccio, A. C. *Organization and Administration of Guidance Services.* Chicago: Rand, McNally, 1962 — $6.00

F. PSYCHOLOGY

*Cole, Luella and Hall, Irma. *Psychology of Adolescence*. (6th ed.) New York: Holt, Rinehart and Winston, 1964 — $7.50

*Cronbach, L. J. *Educational Psychology*. New York: Harcourt, Brace, & World, 1963 — $7.50

*Hilgard, E. R. *Introduction to Psychology*. (3rd ed.) New York: Harcourt, Brace & World, 1962 — $10.75

Jersild, A. T. *The Psychology of Adolescence*. (2nd ed.) New York: MacMillan, 1963 — $6.75

Kelly, W.A. *Educational Psychology*. (Rev. ed.) Milwaukee: Bruce, 1965 — $5.75

Kolesnik, W. B. *Educational Psychology*. New York: McGraw-Hill, 1963 — $7.50

G. EDUCATION IN GENERAL

Boyd, W. *The History of Western Education*. (7th ed.) London: A. and C. Black, 1965 — $5.75

*Brubacher, J.S. *Modern Philosophies of Education*. (3rd ed.) New York: McGraw-Hill, 1962 —$6.95

*Butts, R.F. and Cremin, L. A. *A History of Education in American Culture*. New York: Holt, 1963 — $7.25

Harris, C. W. (ed.) *Encyclopedia of Educational Research*. (3rd ed.) New York: MacMillan, 1960 — $27.50

Maritain, J. *Education at the Crossroads*. New Haven: Yale University, Paperbound, (1943) 1961 — $1.25

Mayer, M. *The Schools*. New York: Harper, 1961 — $5.95

*Nash, A. and Perkinson, H. *The Educated Man: Studies in the History of Educational Thought*. New York: J. Wiley, 1965 — $7.95

H. JOURNALS

College Board Review. College Entrance Examination Board, Publications Order Office, Box 592, Princeton, New Jersey. (quarterly) — *Annual subscription*: $1.00

Insight. 1831 College Ave. Quincy, Ill. (quarterly) — *Annual subscription:* $5.00

Journal of Counseling Psychology. 1945 N. High Street, Columbus, Ohio 43210 (quarterly) — *Annual subscription:* $8.00

National Catholic Guidance Conference Journal. 2401 69th Street, Kenosha, Wisconsin 53140 (quarterly) — *Annual subscription:* $5

Occupational Outlook Quarterly. U.S. Government Printing Office, Washington, D.C. 20402 (quarterly) — *Annual subscription:* $1.25

Personnel and Guidance Journal. 1605 New Hampshire Ave., N.W., Washington, D.C. 20009 (monthly) — *Annual subscription:* $10

The School Counselor. 1605 New Hampshire Ave., N.W., Washington, D.C. 20009 (quarterly) — *Annual subscription:* $4.00

The Vocational Guidance Quarterly. 1605 New Hampshire Ave., N.W., Washington, D.C. 20009 (quarterly) — *Annual subscription:* $3.00

APPENDIX II

SKETCHES OF FLOOR PLANS
OF SOME GUIDANCE SUITES

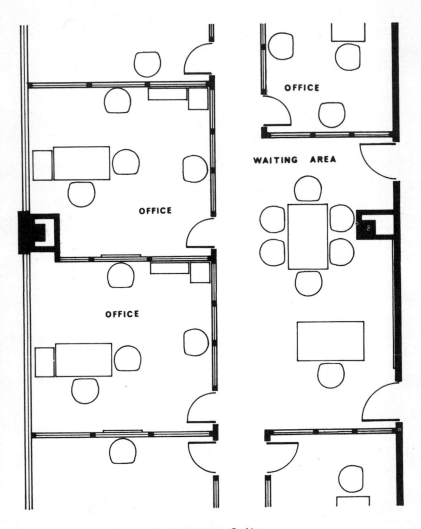

Prototype Plan of Guidance Suite
BOARD of EDUCATION, City of New York

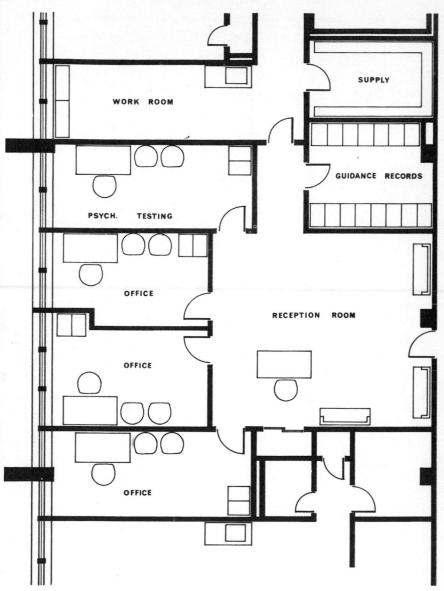

WORK ROOM

SUPPLY

GUIDANCE RECORDS

PSYCH. TESTING

OFFICE

RECEPTION ROOM

OFFICE

CORRIDOR

OFFICE

Floor Plan of Guidance Counseling Suite
EMERSON SCHOOL, Yonkers, New York

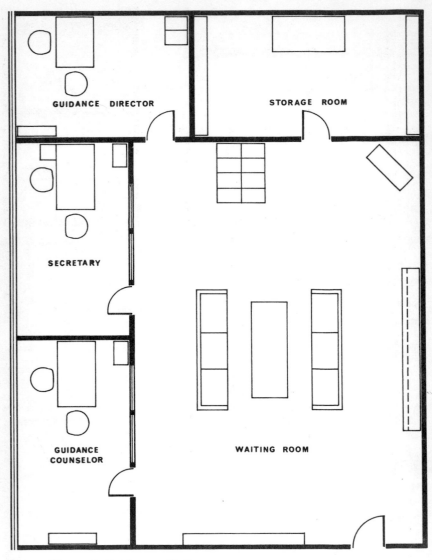

GUIDANCE DIRECTOR

STORAGE ROOM

SECRETARY

GUIDANCE COUNSELOR

WAITING ROOM

Floor Plan of Guidance Suite
CARDINAL SPELLMAN HIGH SCHOOL, Bronx, New York

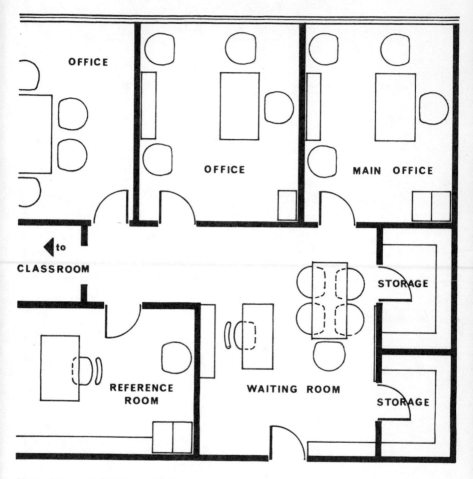

Floor Plan of Guidance Suite
BISHOP REILLY HIGH SCHOOL, Fresh Meadows, New York

DAUGHTERS OF ST. PAUL

IN MASSACHUSETTS
50 St. Paul's Ave.
Jamaica Plain
Boston, Mass. 02130
172 Tremont St.
Boston, Mass. 02111
381 Dorchester St.
So. Boston, Mass. 02127
325 Main St.
Fitchburg, Mass.
IN NEW YORK
78 Fort Place
Staten Island, N.Y. 10301
625 East 187th St.
Bronx, N.Y.
39 Erie St.
Buffalo, N.Y. 14202
IN CONNECTICUT
202 Fairfield Ave.
Bridgeport, Conn. 06603
IN OHIO
141 West Rayen Ave.
Youngstown, Ohio 44503
Daughters of St. Paul
Cleveland, Ohio
IN TEXAS
114 East Main Plaza
San Antonio, Texas 78205
IN CALIFORNIA
1570 Fifth Ave.
San Diego, Calif. 92101
278 - 17th Street
Oakland, California 94612
IN LOUISIANA
86 Bolton Ave.
Alexandria, La. 71301
IN FLORIDA
2700 Biscayne Blvd.
Miami, Florida 33137
IN CANADA
8885 Blvd. Lacordaire
St. Leonard Deport-Maurice
Montreal, Canada
1063 St. Clair Ave. West
Toronto, Canada
IN ENGLAND
29 Beauchamp Place
London, S.W. 3, England
IN AFRICA
Box 4392
Kampala, Uganda
IN INDIA
Water Field Road Extension
Plot No. 143
Bandra, India
IN THE PHILIPPINE ISLANDS
2650 F.B. Harrison St.
Pasay City
Philippine Islands
IN AUSTRALIA
58 Abbotsford Rd.
Homebush N.S.W., Australia
226 Victoria Square
Adelaide, South-Australia
6 Muir Street
Hawthorn, Victoria, Australia